Can the Left Learn to Meme?

Adorno, Video Gaming, and Stranger Things

Can the Left Learn to Meme?

Adorno, Video Gaming, and Stranger Things

Mike Watson

zero books

Winchester, UK
Washington, USA

JOHN HUNT PUBLISHING

First published by Zero Books, 2019
Zero Books is an imprint of John Hunt Publishing Ltd., No. 3 East St., Alresford,
Hampshire SO24 9EE, UK
office@jhpbooks.com
www.johnhuntpublishing.com
www.zero-books.net

For distributor details and how to order please visit the 'Ordering' section on our website.

ISBN: 978 1 78535 723 7
978 1 78535 724 4 (ebook)
Library of Congress Control Number: 2018963356

A CIP catalogue record for this book is available from the British Library.

Design: Stuart Davies

UK: Printed and bound by CPI Group (UK) Ltd, Croydon, CR0 4YY
US: Printed and bound by Thomson-Shore, 7300 West Joy Road, Dexter, MI 48130

Contents

Preface Talking about my generation 1

Chapter 1 Stranger Things: Art and politics—an impossible pairing 5

Chapter 2 In which we find little hope in generational dreaming 14

Chapter 3 In which we find little hope in the art world 29

Chapter 4 Keeping up with the cat memes 46

Chapter 5 In which we find some solace in *Mad Men* 58

Chapter 6 The kids are doing it for themselves: but what is 'it'? 67

Chapter 7 Lessons from the *League* 77

Endnotes 92

References 97

Also by the author

Towards a Conceptual Militancy, Zero Books, 2016
ISBN 978-1-78099-231-0

Preface

Talking about my generation

Every generation is born somewhere in the period between its members' youth and their early adulthood, whether that be a pained labour spent sniffing glue to the punk refrain of 'No Future' in 1977 for UK-born Generation X-ers, or the emergency caesarean birth of 2001 when coming of age millennials on both sides of the Atlantic saw the Twin Towers impossibly collapse in real time on their TV screens. For many generations this point marks the start of a programme to change the world based on some new configuration of hope or despair. Even 'No Future' presaged a new era free both from the pomposities of a class- and capital-driven Britain, and the happy-clappy remedies of the hippy era proposed by Generation X's parents – the Baby Boomers. Punk coincided with postmodern theory, which though assured in its rejection of the cumbersome and naive narratives of the modern era, was somehow taken in by the happy notion of the 'global village'. The formation of the millennial, however, coincided with hope's passing in the aftermath of the Twin Towers' collapse, as western governments embarked on an unprecedented policy of cynicism in international affairs that tore up the dreams of their modern and postmodern forebears.[1]

Accordingly, the millennials' task is to make something positive from the two negative poles of reality – the bleakness of existence and the infeasibility of all our imagined remedies. In this they share at least something in common with an unlikely predecessor; Theodor Wiesengrund Adorno (1906-1969), to whom this book is dedicated. The German sociologist, musicologist and philosopher aimed via his system of 'negative dialectics' to conceive of some small hope even within the bleak world he inhabited as a Jewish exile from Germany, returning in the aftermath of the Second World War. That hope, he argued, would come only rarely and fleetingly to the viewer or listener of modern art which, due to its radical abstraction, could expose the falseness of a society completely beholden to capitalism and its mass media propaganda machine (which Adorno named the 'culture industry'). Today, however, the art world has itself become but a wing of a new virulent strain of finance capital, making recourse to art unrealistic as an opposition to wanton materialism. At the same time art's historical elitism – something Adorno arguably perpetuated in his own time – seems as entrenched as it ever has been.

As such, the millennial arguably needs to look to new forms of communication, which in any case defy many of Adorno's critiques of the media. Memes, online gaming, and social media have opened up boundless opportunities for expression, which while entrenched within the data economy offer the opportunity for perpetual creation and dissemination such that occasional moments of critical incisiveness might gain traction. Rare as these moments are, the Adornian injunction to keep on producing despite the odds stacked against free thought and expression is honoured, perhaps even unwittingly.

Parallel to this there exists a fight being waged for millennials' souls (and electoral votes) as their vast undirected energy, conveyed across the internet on social media, image boards and Massive Online Battle Arenas, is sought by political players such as Steve Bannon, so as to direct it to right-wing ends. Bannon's premise is that the millennial, unchastened by rules and traditions, needs harnessing and putting to work in the service of a conservative revival. What this book proposes, utilising the best of Adorno (his unerring yet understated hope in spite of the odds) against the worst of Adorno (his uncouth cultural elitism), is an embrace of the abstraction of the new media landscape, as millennials refuse to surrender entirely to the cynicism of the markets or of right-wing populism, by outweirding even the world-at-large.

Taking the plot of *Stranger Things* as an analogy, Chapter 1 explores the awkward dyad 'art and politics' and asks if it offers something to aid the path of the 'spiritual-revolutionary' dreamer, as an archetype that has led successive generations, or whether art has become co-opted by the conservative-material forces that perennially blight its course.

Chapter 2 enquires as to whether we can really speak of fixed political generations. If so, what is the inheritance and fate of the millennial? Exploring this question in relation to post-war generations, Adorno's hope in the face of catastrophe, while all the while refusing to find solace in rules and myths, is contrasted to both the militant right-wing approach of Steve Bannon and the conservative psychology of Jordan Peterson – both of which bind the millennial to a rigid sense of duty.

Looking to the late John Berger – the great populariser of leftist art critique – Chapter 3 asks what, if any, hope might reside in contemporary art, with its ingrained elitism. Examining the trajectories of Baby Boomer and millennial artists Jean-Michel Basquiat and Oscar Murillo, we find that the art world is as hopelessly beholden to financial interests as it is tied to age-old racial divides.

Chapters 4 and 5 find that the art world has lost its way since the avant garde dream of an 'art-for-all' was first touted in the nineteenth century. In submitting cultural phenomena as diverse as mid-twentieth-century mass media, the Kardashian-Jenners, cat memes, *Mad Men*, and Run the Jewels to Adornian scrutiny, we find the philosopher to be peculiarly highbrow, and otherwise outmoded. Facing both the philosopher's elitism and the massive gap between cultural production today and in the post-war period, it is argued that Adorno's most enduring and endearing theoretical device is the possibility he holds for creative abstraction in undermining the false conditions of a capitalist society via the 'shudder' it evokes in the viewer.

This shudder, a device that runs throughout Adorno's work, temporarily shocks the viewer out of their acceptance of a society completely beholden to capital.

In chapters 6 and 7, that shudder is located in Vaporwave music, homemade YouTube series' such as *Don't Hug Me I'm Scared* and online gaming. Examining Adorno's wider motives for favouring abstraction it is argued that capitalism is founded on false predicates applied to nature so as to minimise the latter's threat. This process of 'identity thinking' can only be overturned via novel creative output, which radically throws into question the falsity of an overzealous process of rationalisation. Returning to Steve Bannon and Jordan Peterson, it will be argued that their reasoning fails precisely because of their desire to reinstate a perceived golden age of 'order', whereas it is arguably the ordering principles of capital (as a rationalisation gone awry) that threaten stability in the world as it routinely teeters over into authoritarianism. While Adorno cannot have foreseen the extent to which society itself would become both radically abstract and pluralist, or the degree to which media would become user oriented, there remains hope for the left in the counter-rationalist tendency of creative production that he espoused.

Finally, this book is indebted to the growing presence of a virulent online left that operates across YouTube, Twitter, Facebook, Instagram and Reddit. The growth of the specifically 'online' left, as it attempts to counter the online right via memes, videos and discussion provides a significant contribution to the internet as a medium that in any case threatens to destabilise an administered society. Here I describe what may be achieved by embracing the wayward and unpredictable tendencies of the internet as a whole. Within this the left internet has a particular role in campaigning and directing policy discussion.

Chapter 1

Stranger Things: Art and politics—an impossible pairing

The hit franchise *Stranger Things* (Netflix, 2016, 2017, and 2019) revolves around a battle to free the hapless 13-year-old Will Byers from the clutches of the monstrous ''Mindflayer'', an underworld demon which eventually comes to possess him. Set in the small fictional town of Hawkins, Indiana, where nothing much usually happens, series one of *Stranger Things* focuses on the initial disappearance of Will Byers, and his Mom, Joyce Byers', refusal to accept that he is dead even when a body is apparently found. Joyce (played by Winona Ryder) is rewarded for her stubbornness when Will is found to be alive, albeit trapped in a dark mirror of our own world, called the Upside Down — which is somehow linked to the secretive Hawkins National Laboratory, a military research centre. What is unclear in both series one and series two is the extent to which Will's detachment from 'reality' (appearing eerily distant from his peers even when he's with them) might be part-psychological. An awkward and shy teenager of clearly high intelligence, there appears by analogy to be more to Will's sociopathy than mere demon possession (or indeed, is the demon possession analogous of psychological malaise?). The Upside Down — a kind of dark gloopy mirror of our world populated by monsters that take their energy from the central Demogorgon — is staved off only temporarily for Will, suggesting an innate personal discord with reality. His neurosis, psychosis even, brings glimpses of an untamed and fitful nature to which he, his kin and his village neighbours are bound despite the widespread repression of this fact. By the start of series two, Will's disappearance and return has been all but forgotten by the townspeople, even though several of them experienced the dark landscape of the Upside Down, with some even having battled the Demogorgon – a monstrous bipedal creature who stalks the inhabitants of Hawkins.. Despite knowing of the existence of this underworld, the townsfolk of Hawkins prefer to blind themselves to it through the maintenance of a safe, small-town existence, until things begin to go awry once again.

In the first episode of *Stranger Things Two* we see Will in a gaming arcade with close friends Mike, Dustin and Lucas, playing the cult classic *Dragon's Lair* (1983), as he turns to see that it is snowing outside. Upon turning back to ask his friends if they too see the snow, the scene both inside and outside the arcade morphs into the Upside Down, which appears for Will as superimposed on the real world, so as to replace its features with a kind of hellish substitute devoid of other people, and dripping with dark slime and organic entrails. Venturing outside the arcade Will's gaze, which has by now become a thousand-yard stare, fixes on the stormy sky, which flashes red with a diabolic electric storm. Given Will's sensitivity and prior close brush with the Upside Down this appears as the first sign that, once again, all is not well in Hawkins, Indiana. Will suddenly returns to normalcy when Mike calls him back inside to take his turn on the video game *Dig Dug*, wherein the central character digs his way through an underground world, battling monsters along the way. While Will's visions are put down to PTSD by a doctor who is employed by Hawkins National Laboratory, it is clear to the viewer that they portend calamity, and one greater than befell Hawkins' residents back in series one (otherwise why make a sequel, right?). Will continues to see disturbing visions that appear to make him physically ill, and which he attempts to process by drawing them. At one point in episode four he begins to frantically scribble page upon page of seemingly random abstractions. In blue and black hatch marks upon the white background of the paper, they appear as tens of angry preludes to action-paintings, not unlike the work of Jackson Pollock or Willem de Kooning. Taken perhaps as evidence that Will is indeed suffering psychological trauma, the drawings are pieced together by Joyce Byers and local chief of police Hopper, who realise that the seemingly random expressionist drawings actually form a map, perhaps of the troubling vine growths that had recently plagued local pumpkin fields. One episode later, Joyce's boyfriend, Bob Newby, aids Joyce and Will in reading the map, which actually charts a series of underground tunnels where Hopper was by now trapped in a mesh of vines. Here we see a classic case of seemingly random creativity yield truths that otherwise remain hidden. Will, who is actually in continual commune with the Mindflayer after the latter left itself partially embedded in him at the end of series one (unbeknownst to Will or the viewer at the time), appears to be the intermediary between 'reality' and the falsity that most people around him choose to inhabit. The apparent obviousness that something is afoot at the military laboratory that covertly operates beneath residents' noses can only be brought to the fore by artistic abstractions that are unsettling enough to temporarily jilt the viewer into a realisation of the 'truth': our fragile day to day routines of living only barely hide the dark reality that we are being manipulated by a military-industrial complex that hides just beneath the surface of everyday life. Or more accurately, *it is embedded within it*. What *Stranger Things* conveys so well, is that one is only ever — speaking analogously — either in the darkness looking out of it (and perhaps warning people not to 'go there' themselves) or in the light trying hard to ignore the darkness that was the very motive for creating the light (perhaps we could say 'artificial illumination') in the first place. What the organic rotten mulch-like aesthetic of the Upside Down conveys above all is the coexistence of nature as a kind of first tyranny, which will inevitably deliver us unto death, only thinly distanced from a second tyranny, which humanity erected to counter nature's threat. The military-scientific compound, with its experiments-gone-awry, represents that second tyranny.

In the 'reaching out' of the Hawkins' townsfolk for a stable reality that remains ever elusive — or towards a chaotic 'truth' that must be confronted — one can find comparison with the real-world failure of society to deliver on the idealistic promises of early modernism, or indeed the pre-modern Judeo-Christian period. The lure of an imagined transcendent realm has spurred on many generations. Today, for better or worse, such dreams appear naive, though the popularity of televised or filmic fantasy and nostalgia (*Stranger Things* owes much to '80s classics *E.T.* and *Stand by Me*) suggests we are far from done with dreaming in itself. Indeed, the level of creative output being published on a day-to-day basis — as seen in meme production, instant messaging and the sharing of video clip diaries on Instagram and Snapchat — is unprecedented. Tragi-comically, the millennial generation, lacking the utopian vision of many of its modernist forebears, partakes more than any previous generation in the avant garde dream of a democratisation of creative output and reception. Meanwhile any prophesied attendant political awakening seems as distant as it ever has been. The freedom to creatively share information and resources more widely than ever before on the global stage has not transpired, for example, in a communist youth movement. Flashes of dissidence aside (the Arab Spring and Occupy come to mind), the young have all but given up on utopia. And yet somewhere out there resides an imagined otherness that the millennial wishes to be delivered to or from. For Adorno any such hope would likely involve art and its tenuous link to politics.

The pairing 'art and politics' has since the post-war period been an area for intense debate. Art, the realm that can dream anything but act on nothing, cannot by definition ever truly meet with politics, a realm that has the potential to act yet is blocked by real-world practicalities. A politics that can act upon art's

dreams is arguably the basis of the leftist modernist enterprise, though it has historically been tragically blighted (as can be seen in the historical course and fate of Russian and Chinese communism). Emerging generations arguably have no need to explore for themselves the possibilities offered by a politicised art on the one hand, and an 'art-ified' politics on the other. History speaks plainly of the failings of this project. It is perhaps for this reason that the Sanders and Corbyn movements appear – for good or bad – peculiarly centrist and practical when put in historical perspective.

Perhaps one difficulty in achieving a successful pairing between the polar opposites of a creative political 'dream' and concrete 'reality' resides in their concomitance as much as their absolute difference. The path of the imagination is necessary to the revolutionary path, though the latter depends on a discipline more associated with the conservatism of the formal political path. A meeting between the revolutionary and dreamlike path and the conservative and materialistic path cannot bear fruit as both paths lead on their own to nowhere. That is to say, while the concrete political path comes up against the resistance of reality (and of myriad oppositions to its every proposal), the artistic path only succeeds inasmuch as it is not real, meaning that even its most lucid imaginings must come to nothing. Something of this dilemma was seen by Adorno, who in 1969 refused to support protests organised by his students in Germany on the basis that they were doomed to repeat the perennial mistakes of their forebears. So long, Adorno argued, as human thought was fundamentally skewed towards the tendency to control both nature and other humans, the leap towards any imagined utopia would flounder. As such, any idea of deliverance from a society irrevocably beholden to capital had to be grounded in the impossibility of its conditions, otherwise it would risk becoming another disastrous attempt at revolution in the mould of Nazism or Soviet Communism (an example of the 'second tyranny' spoken of above, which Adorno termed 'second nature'). Only by first confronting and questioning our tendency to try to control the risks posed by nature by drawing a false binary between us and the world-at-large, might we escape a cycle of revolution descending into tyranny. If art has a place in this, it resides in its refusal to conform to a wayward system of rationality that attempts to cajole reality into conforming to the human desire to comfort.

Whether wittingly or not, such refusal to be carried away by the dreams of their forebears arguably underlays the cynicism of millennials today. This can be seen when we consider that even the societal dreams that have been realised — via technological and mediatic advance rather than political headway — have failed to deliver on their imagined promise. Writing in the US, Adorno himself was a central figure in the critique of mass media — what he termed the 'culture industry'— arguing that the mass-produced media products of the mid-twentieth century presented samey offerings posing as a myriad of free choices, leaving a passive public receptive to the capitalist propaganda that they purchased.[2] That being the case, there might be cause for positivity today when the public is as likely to produce media as to be the audience for it. Indeed, if the avant garde of the Post Impressionists, Dadaists and Surrealists aimed at a progressive horizontalism in the arts (achieved via a consideration of everyday scenes, objects and thought processes), surely social media presents a triumph that goes beyond our forebears' wildest imaginings?

Tragically, no. The dream of cultural democracy has had to reckon with two complicating factors: counter democratic forces (be they corporate or governmental) and democracy itself. With regard to the former, legislation and legal infringements have led to a situation whereby our freedom of expression can be monitored, sold as data and potentially held against us, as seen with the Snowden leaks. In the latter case of 'democracy', something tending towards absolute freedom to make and share content has resulted in the wide proliferation of selfie images, cat videos, pornography and very little comparatively in the way of revolutionary strategising. Perhaps – who knows? – it's a position that early modern and avant garde artists such as Cézanne, Buñuel and Duchamp might have countenanced, yet its equivalent political effect, in the form of a far-right movement fuelled by cruel in-jokes and Nazi-imagery distributed over internet message boards and social media, feels far from the political modernism of revolutionary communism.

The masses, given potentially more freedom to communicate than ever before, have tended towards a categorisation and control of their own image via selfies, other personalised images (of products, memorabilia, etc), and memes aimed at shoring up their identity. This would not perhaps have surprised Adorno, who might have argued that the negative tendency to categorise people and objects (what he called 'identity thinking') will be present in our actions until we successfully rethink thought itself. This tendency, which is aimed at understanding the world so that we can better live in it, all too often leads us to control the world, with often disastrous consequences, including war, climate change and genocide.

The selfie is an act of self-categorisation (or 'identification') which while aimed at marking out a territory for individual action and freedom actually leaves its protagonist dumb and lock-jawed at the end of a mass-produced selfie stick. Indeed, we know either from personal experience or observation that shared images of spontaneity (the identification of freedom in ourselves) are often the result of the laboured repetition of a pose repeated until it's 'just right'. Its effects are banal in comparison to the disasters wrought by the military and industrial complex, though the selfie's effect of control is certainly potent. Globally, it has done arguably more to make women conform to a certain ideal of beauty than any governmental edict.

Despite his cynicism, Adorno called for a continuation of art production, even given the impossibility of it challenging the dominance of capital, such that its continued existence resists total surrender to cynicism.

> The question asked by a character in Sartre's play Morts Sans Sepulture, 'Is there any meaning in life when men exist who beat people until the bones break in their bodies?', is also the question whether any art now has a right to exist; whether intellectual regression is not inherent in the concept of committed literature because of the regression of society. But Enzensberger's retort also remains true, that literature must resist this verdict, in other words, be such that its mere existence after Auschwitz is not a surrender to cynicism.[3]

And it is perhaps this refusal to succumb to cynicism that we are witnessing in the perpetual production of internet memes by the millennial generation and, increasingly, their successors (for now tentatively named 'Generation Y'), however 'cynical' in message they may themselves at times be.

'Art and politics' might have failed us, as what we could term the 'spiritual-revolutionary' path of the dreamer has found itself sold out to the 'materialist-conservative' one of the politician or financier. The former aims at radical change in the self and society, the latter towards a maintenance of stability through material wealth. As such, the millennial has little choice but to carry on producing cultural objects (be they memes, viral videos or selfies) from a perspective of loss. Loss of the dream of a radical break with the drudgery of political domination at the hands of capital. And yet within this, at some point one has to admit there is a level of mediatic 'choice' incomparable with that enjoyed by millennials' predecessors, albeit within a society that is capitalist beyond challenge.

What Adorno advocated was the creation of an abstract art capable of momentarily transcending the tendency to 'identify' and thus nullify the world around. This identification was embodied by the glib output of the culture industry (best exemplified in Hollywood movies, elevator music and trashy magazines). Adorno felt, somewhat naively perhaps, that the abstraction of, for example, a Samuel Beckett play or Kafka novel might snap us out of the complacency induced by an exposure to corporate mulch, which itself arises from the abstraction of capitalism (that reduces all things to numbers). By way of analogy we might see this abstraction embodied in Will Byers' scribblings, which cut through the falsity of the small-town idyll that many of his elders and peers want to believe in, as well as the deceptions peddled by the military-industrial outpost on his doorstep.

Though what Adorno could not foresee is the wider abstraction wrought by the sheer speed of cultural output we witness daily in the twenty-first century. That is to say, that for Adorno mid-twentieth century capitalism was a form of abstraction that posed as rational, necessitating a further abstraction to expose its fallacy, whereas today there is barely any pretence to rationalism. We appear to have succumbed entirely to abstraction.

Within the abstraction of dissonant images and sounds bearing down on us, the selfie, the meme, the YouTube video and the indie video game perhaps represent an attempt to match the madness of our media world either through interaction with its absurdity or by temporarily staving off a safe (and wholly fabricated) space within it. It's a half empty-cup mentality that doesn't expect to become full on the basis of the fulfilment of prophecy (political or religious). Freedom, agency, creativity — call it what you will — will have to come about via an interaction with the world of things that comes most readily to hand. Most often that's a smartphone, tablet or PC.

Chapter 2

In which we find little hope in generational dreaming

Before we get onto the possibility of creative deliverance from human-made tyranny, it is worth taking time to consider whether there is any sense talking about millennials – or indeed, generations – at all. Having done this, we will ascertain the extent to which artistic endeavour might be an effective path today in exposing the 'falsity' of prevailing social conditions.

A millennial can have been born anywhere between 1977 and 1982, according to which time frame one subscribes to. This gap is not insignificant as it means that the oldest millennials can have been anywhere between 9 and 14 years of age when Nirvana's *Nevermind* went to the top of the US billboard chart, suggesting that they were either blissfully ignorant, playing with dolls or making camps in the garden, or were experimenting with blue rinses, bleach and smoking weed.

While generational boundaries are clearly decidedly slippery, there are some clear consistencies in generational theory. For example, most millennials will have experienced the early stages of dating as a largely online phenomena, conducted via smartphones and SMS and employing emoticons to convey pathos. It is unlikely that anyone from Generation X can say the same. Indeed, the whole process of building relationships of any kind, from familial bonds to friendship groups, to romantic or sexual relations has changed profoundly from Generation X to the millennial generation.

As a gauge of the gulf in human socialisation from one generation to the next, the 1995 cult film *Empire Records* (directed by Allan Moyle), set around a soon to close independent record store and the group of kooky late Gen-Xers that frequent it, would be implausible in the twenty-first century.

The strength of the bonds made between its central characters (who include Liv Tyler as Corey Mason, Renée Zellweger as Gina and Rory Cochrane as Lucas) would be near impossible today, and would render the central premise – of a bunch of kids rallying around to save their workplace and favourite hangout – redundant if set in the 2010s. The film flopped upon its initial release, possibly due to its dialogue seeming banal at the time. Though it is perhaps the sometimes droll, sometimes whacky conversations between its main characters that have made the film a cult hit on Netflix and Amazon Prime in the last 2 years. This can be seen clearly in the closing scene and conversation (between Mark, played by Ethan Randall, and stoner Eddie, played by James 'Kino' Wills):

Eddie: I admit, Henry Rollins is sort of a puss.

Mark: Yeah, he's a total puss. His lyrics suck.

Eddie: But you can't go and put down the Misfits. They had everything it took to be a great punk band. They had good bass lines and strong guitar chords…even though they were only three.

Mark: They didn't even compare to Primus. They were that old school stuff.

Eddie: Why get into Primus? Primus sucks.

Mark: Primus is the new stuff. Out with the old, in with the new.

Religion's a bad thing if Primus is what's gonna come around.

Eddie: What are you talking about? – The fact that Primus has nothing.Mark: They got good bass lines. I'll admit.

Eddie: They have beautiful bass lines. Six-string fretless bass…

Mark: Okay, but they're not as good as the Pixies.

Eddie: The Pixies have way better bass lines than Primus.

Mark: So why didn't they stick around?

Eddie: Because people wanted to do solo careers and explore themselves...as single entities instead of a band.
Mark: But that's like money.
Eddie: No, it's not about money.
What are you talking about, 'money'?

The conversation takes place outside the closed record shop after a successful party held to save the store at the last minute – and promoted using Xerox'd flyers. With the money raised and Liv Tyler paired up with AJ (played by Johnny Whitworth, best known for his role in the 2017 *Ghostrider*), Mark and Eddie are left to talk into the small hours, about everything – and mostly nothing. For Generation X viewers there is something jarring in hearing Primus being called the 'new thing'. Even in 1995 they were relatively seasoned as an act, having been formed in 1984. Though what really jilts those of us who recall the '90s is the loss of an era in which conversations could just meander, and the importance this had in building friendship bonds. Somehow, the freedom offered by mobile and internet communications has led to a difficulty in choosing one's words, as the speed and intensity of communication flattens everything out into a kind of lowest common denominator of dialogue. This arguably echoes Adorno's famed declaration that it is impossible to write lyric poetry after Auschwitz, as the conditions for reflection had been superseded by total control at the hands of capital. It would appear that the ubiquity of image and audio objects render it impossible to say anything as such. We have been entrapped by a system of information exchange that was supposed to set us free. It is perhaps the desire to escape this that explains the popularity of nostalgia-based offerings on Netflix, with several series released in the period 2016-2018 featuring cultural references relevant to Generation X (including *Stranger Things*, *The Get Down*, *GLOW* and the second series of *Dear White People*, featuring flashbacks to several decades, including the '70s and '80s).

The Getdown (2016), set in the '70s Bronx, charts the rise of hip-hop and disco music through a criminal underworld where drugs and bootleg recordings fuel a fast-growing music scene that acts as a pressure valve for the Bronx's racial tensions. Here, solace is found in a nostalgia for a time that was perhaps no simpler than our own. Yet it is in any case a time that is now long gone, meaning the viewer momentarily avoids the difficulty (or responsibility) of talking or thinking about race in the present. Though ultimately, the solace provided by the warm buzz of nostalgia or the emotional protection offered by black humour is fleeting. Sooner or later the real world must be negotiated. Though how much is this desire to escape specific to generation (if at all)? And should we take generational theories seriously in any case?

Going beyond tit-for-tat bickering between family members, generational politics has arguably been a crucial feature in the political landscape since the rise of mass media, which has made people more aware of their own generational traits and therefore more able to make demands as a group defined by proximity of birth date. For a generation to knowingly exist its members must be able to identify shared experiences that take place at a similar point in their lives, the effects of which play out over time in consistent ways. For example, the Twin Towers attack will have had a very different effect on someone aged between, say, 5 and 20 in comparison with someone aged 60 to 75 at the time. The younger person may have undergone a great shift in their vision of planes, and of towers, seeing a world that had become unpredictable and hostile in new and evolving ways. The older person perhaps saw a continuation of a tendency towards attacks on US targets by probably Islamic operatives as a response to an arguably questionable US foreign policy, and a continued propensity towards violence in a world that is never fully at peace. Quite clearly there exist attitudes, hopes and fears that are relative to the age at which people experience given historical events. This is what defines a 'generation'.

Yet beyond actually having a history and experience rooted in a specific time period, generations need to be aware of their 'shared experience': i.e. of the existence of other people of a similar age that see the world in broadly similar terms. The novel, the magazine, newspaper, TV film and, today, the internet have clearly played a role in forging this sense of a collective generational identity. Without a media capable of joining people together across distances it is impossible to know on any individual level to what extent shared attitudes with one's peers are due to generational rather than, for example, class and gender factors. For sure we tend to disagree with our elders, but that can be explained away by differences in the attitudes of age cohorts. For example, while your parents admonish (or once admonished) their children for playing loud music past a certain hour, so did *theirs*. Generation X, the Baby Boomers and even the 'Silent' Generation (with its love of the moral panic inducing genres of jazz and swing) were all once chastised for the volume of their music. What the media does is make us aware that the particular form of chastisement and rebellion we experience is unique to our generation, forming a sense of tribalism necessitating special equipment that must be purchased (such as cosmetics, video games, baseball caps, etc.).

Hand-in-hand with an increased awareness of generation due to mass-produced media comes a belief in the right to undergo a phase of self-discovery between childhood and adulthood. Such a period of socialisation contributes to an awareness of neither being an adult bearing the responsibility of family and civic duty, or a child shaped in the parental self-image. This phenomenon came about in post-depression America due to a new-found financial independence on the part of pre-adults, which was quickly exploited by marketers and the media.[4]

The teenage years are marked partly by the individual

adolescent's awareness of their difference from their elders. Though this is not just the difference experienced as a child who is aware of the existence of diverse age groups (that of their parents and teachers and that of their grandparents, for example). Over time the young person starts to understand that all their elders were once their own age, but none of them belonged to their own generation. And in that realisation there begins a lifelong membership of a tribe comprising diverse yet shared symbols and codes. These symbols and codes – such as hairstyles, music, slang, use of gadgetry – provide the framework within which the aspirations of youth are played out and also one within which products are designed and marketed. These frameworks in turn arguably characterise the political desires and cultural preferences of a given generation throughout adulthood, as optimism gives way to realism. Such a process marks the formulation of a generation's identity, as the archetype of the artist or rebel figure is seized upon. This pattern can be seen in filmic portrayals of high school and teen upstarts (from *Rebel Without a Cause*, to *Grease*, *Ferris Bueller's Day Off*, to *Heathers*, to *The Babysitter*). Typically, a generation starts out on a quest for creative assertion or rebellion, with the aim being to reconfigure the space they operate within: the high school, the suburban town one is born into, etc. What ensues is some more or less committed following of a spiritual-revolutionary path, set inevitably on a course to failure as each generation reckons with the conservative and materialist forces that shape society.[5]

To briefly trace a history of recent generations, the GI (or 'greatest') generation, which preceded the Baby Boomers, encountered both the Great Depression and the Second World War. While being war weary they were, at least in allied countries, proud of their survival through adversity and universally keen to build a new stable world. They were characterised by principles of steadfastness in adversity, duty, trustworthiness and religious faith. Their most radical element

— the 'beats' or 'beatniks' — proposed no political programme as such, but rather a path of self-development characterised by increased spiritual, ecological and sexual awareness. For such a movement to become incendiary required the disillusionment brought about by the Vietnam War. Effectively, the injection of violence (and a spirited opposition to it) into the heady but languid torpor of sex and drugs.

If the first hippies were in fact late era beatniks, the transformation from a kind of post-war ritual of spiritual self-knowledge to a counter-government movement was made possible by a radically changed world, with an increasingly young demographic of 'Baby Boomers'.[6] It was a world where the sexual and spiritual exploration of the beats met with the concrete political tendencies of the Lost and G.I Generations, who had come before them. However, they did not by any means find complete agreement with the Baby Boomers' demands. In France a contrast between the G.I and Lost Generation, and the Baby Boomers emerged as the workers' unions failed to see the value of the student movement of 1968, which might otherwise have overthrown De Gaulle's Presidency. Central to the 1968 uprisings was discontent at a university system which was unable to adapt to changing times and the quadrupling of student numbers between 1950 and 1968. This shift in university demographics, from upper- to lower-middle class meant that the university was unresponsive to the needs of students that did not come from academic backgrounds. All in all, while both the GI and Baby Boomer generations wanted a better world, the latter kicked against the authority (embodied in a figure like De Gaulle) that the former saw as central to political and economic stability. It is common for conservatives to misread this historical situation and to argue that a perceived decadence in today's society arose from the disdain for authority of the Baby Boomer generation. Indeed this is the argument put forth by Steve Bannon in his documentary *Generation Zero* (2010), which was strongly influenced by the generational theory of Strauss-Howe, as is shortly to be discussed. For now, it is enough to say that it is arguably a tendency towards too much control that we need be wary of, and not its opposite.[7]

For Generation X (approximately 1960 to 1980), free love and LSD evoke little other than alimony and drug psychosis. While a mantra of peace and love provided a neat soundbite for the anti-war movement, the propensity for the powerful to consolidate their position at the expense of others was clearly not in any decline. Love had not transformed politics. Hippy visionaries became tech company tycoons as Reagan and Thatcher began to pursue a vision of a world governed by capital, with governments existing merely to clear the path for financial interests to prosper. With the fall of the Soviet Union and the birth of George Bush Senior's New World Order signalling American hegemony, the US military and its allies became a kind of worldwide sheriff: a position consolidated by George Bush Junior via his declaration of a 'War on Terror'. Conflict became highly mobile, perpetual and only thinly presaged on any ethical concern. Generation X responded with a pragmatic approach: if the politicians weren't going to do politics conventionally, neither would they. In a world run by increasingly lightweight governments who pushed corporate interests onto the public via the mass media, media and corporations would become the battleground.

Initiatives such as Live Aid, the 1985 concert held across 150 nations to raise money for African famine, acknowledged the failure of Woodstock some 16 years earlier to heal the world. Unfortunately, no amount of government lobbying would help either, hence a kind of DIY humanitarian response, built on punk's incredulity towards authority yet admixed with the media savvy of Baby Boomer Bob Geldof — who somehow achieved lasting fame on the back of his 1979 New Wave hit 'I don't like Mondays' — and his music world friends. Staying true to this form, the remainder of the '80s and '90s was a time of intense political awareness, of brand boycotts, of Adbusting, of 'No Logo' (Naomi Klein's seminal text on new imperialism and the evils of fashion branding) and — despite all this knowing dissent — of corporate power being consolidated like never before. It didn't seem to matter that Generation X-ers had diluted hope down to its weakest possible concoction. The system flushed it away all the same.

Africa is now being bought up and covertly fought over in the race to secure cobalt for lithium batteries for consumer devices and electric cars optimistically produced to combat global warming.[8] Meanwhile famine and war are leading people to make a dangerous journey across the water to Italy, where they risk being apprehended in Libya and sold as slaves. We see glimpses of this through the media but mostly we are ignorant, as we are ignorant of what is happening in Syria, and of the almost forgotten war in Afghanistan, where soldiers who were not born at the conflict's start will soon start tours of duty. The media have learned to filter out anything that would genuinely rile us, in terms of conflict. But if there really is a nail in the coffin for the media and consumer savvy expectations of Generation X, it's perhaps the extent to which corporations willingly parody their best intentions.

Take the much-maligned Kendall Jenner Pepsi advert of 2017, which saw Kim Kardashian West's half-sister publicise Pepsi by simpering around at the head of an unspecified apparently left-wing rally, to then calm tensions with the police by handing one impossibly handsome officer a can of America's second most loved cola. The advert was derided the world over, but that doesn't matter as the damage had already been done long ago: consumer protest was in any case a poor cover for the fact that the left had run out of space for manoeuvre in the macro-political arena.

We have seen that generations can be said to exist, that they are all more or less hapless in their pursuit of a better world, and that their teen years are crucially formative.

Cue the millennials, who to their credit are as unlikely to be taken in by the claims of consumer protest or ad busting as they are by the mass media itself. Though in that case what exactly do they believe? Well, their instinctive rejection of everything — all their forebears fought for and against — could be described as a stance in itself.

The ambiguity of this stance comes at a price: millennials are either seen as upright yet insipid citizens who shun drugs, free love and parties for economic and domestic stability, or as dangerous sociopaths, incapable of human love and fixated on their social media or internet gaming image. This has led them to be co-opted to widely varying causes, by political actors such as Steve Bannon, who as President Trump's chief strategist built a policy based on crank generational theory: the notion of 'The Fourth Turning', conceived by right-wing cultural commentators William Strauss and Neil Howe in *The Fourth Turning: An American Prophecy - What the Cycles of History Tell Us About America's Next Rendezvous with Destiny*. In the book, published in 1997, the co-authors hypothesise that American history is characterised by cyclical sequences of four 20-year periods called 'turnings', the fourth of which corresponds every 80 years with a great upheaval (such as the Great Depression of 1929). How this upheaval is dealt with depends both upon which generation politically manages the crisis and which is ascendant during the crisis and its aftermath.

Leaving aside the myopic social science behind the Strauss-Howe Generational Theory, the characterisation of millennials as either the saviours or wreckers of society has had a huge influence on the political scene. For Bannon, the event that marked the apex of 'the fourth turning' was the economic crisis of 2008, leaving millennials to either sit tight and make do or to drive the wrecking ball further, such that it might completely destroy the neoliberal world erected by the Baby Boomers and

Generation X (including respectively, Bill Clinton and Barack Obama), together with a good part of the world in general. Seemingly it is the wrecking ball strategy that Bannon chooses for the millennial, but only so as to reinstate a world of trade tariffs, monoculturalism and conservative values.[9] Once out of office he sought to inflame tensions in Europe by forming a foundation – entitled 'The Movement' – aimed at supporting far-right populism across the continent. Though perhaps what he misunderstood is the capacity for the millennial – and, indeed, the wider electorate – to flow along with a world that follows no one model. The right and left are wholly unpredictable, a point Bannon felt sharply as he was largely shunned by the European right during the EU elections of May 2019. Meanwhile, he never envisaged the extent to which a bold new leftist trend in meme and YouTube video making would emerge, countering the right and bolstering Sanders' and Corbyn's ambitions. The macro level impact of this emergent movement, often called 'LeftTube' or 'BreadTube', is yet to be seen, though marginal victories by the left in both Finnish and Spanish General Elections in early 2019 suggest there is everything to fight for still. Most tellingly, it is Bannon's vision of millennials as plugged in sociopaths, and not as upright citizens, that makes them ideal in his mind for the rebuilding of America and Europe. Failure in Bannon's mind would seemingly come about if the upcoming generation is not as zombie-like as he thinks they are.

To backtrack and add another level of complexity to their theory, Strauss and Howe argue that generations conform to archetypes: Prophets, Nomads, Heroes and Artists. It is the hero generation that endures the crisis cycle while the artist begins dreaming and rebuilding. Such an overgeneralisation says much of Strauss and Howe's motives. Both worked as political aides in Washington before becoming cultural commentators and both understood how much both the public and policy makers need clear worldviews that can act as an affirmation that America would triumph over history, through thick and thin. Indeed, the notion that disaster awaits, but that it'll all be alright in the end has been making for compelling copy since at least the Old Testament. That said, the figure of the artist should be seen as significant in the development of a given historical period, just not for the reasons Strauss and Howe state, and not necessarily in any traditional sense of the word 'artist', as will be shortly argued.

The subject of generation has also been at the forefront of another prominent theorist's work, leading to animated online debate, often among millennials themselves. Jordan Peterson's bestselling *12 Rules for Life* (2018) starts out with the premise that what the millennial lacks is a grounding in archetypes, myths and rules for living. Subtitled *An Antidote to Chaos* and reading equally as a societal critique and self-help book, the text prescribes a familiarity with the myths that underpin society as a means to gain back control for a lost generation. This, coupled with some solid 'pull up your socks' advice on confronting the hardships of life, amounts to a rolling back of the cultural and ethical permissiveness engendered by the late modern and postmodern project. The tendency of the Enlightenment Project to proceed in its latter stages not by the accumulation of knowledge but by the renunciation of cold hard facts may for sure have led to an ontological insecurity coming to the fore within college campus culture in the form of 'trigger warnings' and 'safe spaces'.

The buggeration warning is a notice given by a professor to an individual or student group ahead of a course or lesson, lest a student might have a trauma awoken by learning materials. The safe space instead is a space laid out so as to give students a sense of security, into which they can retreat in times of fear or angst. Such coddled young beings are reacting, according to Peterson, to the overbearing presence of chaos in today's world. However, there is a fault in the Canadian psychologist's thesis.

Namely, it would appear to be precisely too much protection from chaos that makes the millennial (and many of their elders) so unprepared for the reality of a universe that refuses to conform to our modern and pre-modern desire for order. Chaos, Peterson says, arises with the interruption of a plan being laid out, such as when the brakes suddenly fail on your automobile, when you discover your partner is cheating or when the taxman audits your accounts.[10] However, what is actually arguably being described here is the eruption of reality into a false world of denial and control. Accordingly, what the millennial needs is less control and more acceptance of a fundamentally recalcitrant natural order. It is our notions of order and of binary models of 'right' and 'wrong' – shored up by ancient and modern myths – that are false, as increasingly borne out by a media culture that is no longer subject to the authoritative control of the State and big business. Such a fact – of there being no truth other than the falsity of our imposed models of understanding – is difficult to countenance. Yet elsewhere Peterson teaches that we shouldn't shy away from difficult things. So why teach the millennial to find solace in myth, rather than confront the base level of chaos present in the universe?[11] It is precisely this false sense of order that Adorno aimed his social critique at, pre-empting postmodernism in his suspicion of absolute knowledge and his recourse to the abstraction of late modern art as a means of countering the staid rationality of capitalist society.

To take distance from the trendy online bashing of Peterson as a moralising reactionary, it is not his head-on engagement with issues of ethics that I take issue with here. Both he and Strauss and Howe are correct to identify a societal problem with long held rigid moral systems. Though arguably we really suffer as a result of being unable to jettison these age-old certainties, and not because we have moved too far from them. For this reason the Peterson who says that we need to have one foot in the realm of order and the other in that of chaos is far more palatable than the one who, in the same book, tells us to 'stand up straight' and 'tidy our rooms'. To be sure Adorno himself was highly contradictory in his overall message, alternating between a cultural permissiveness in his appreciation of experimental music and literature and his disdain for the emerging trends of jazz, glossy magazines and horoscope columns (to name but a few examples). Whether a case of generational misunderstanding or class snobbery, Adorno's ire was always focused on the false order promoted by capitalist industry. Today we are as unlikely as ever to overcome that order by hanging on to an old order, with its attendant rules and myths.

The premise of this book is that, with the exception of the millennial generation, each generation has been characterised by a dream — of stability, of freedom, of the overthrow of hierarchy — only to see that dream blighted due to real-world practicalities. Perhaps this 'burnout' explains the hold that hapless dreamers and artist-figures such as Van Gogh and Jean-Michel Basquiat have over our collective imaginations.

For Adorno, as bleak as Bannon in outlook — though infinitesimally more credible as a thinker — the modern artist provided a means of challenging the staid processes of rationalism, which have resulted in a world dominated by financial interests, but also at a point by the disastrous ordering principles of Leninism and later Stalinism. There was something, he argued, in the irrationality of art that can challenge the negative aspects of capitalism (and other forms of domination) by offering fleeting glimpses of 'truth'. The trouble is that the art world has, in the 50 years since Adorno passed away, become inextricably linked with finance, while remaining as culturally elitist as it always was (a point that Adorno's high social class position led him to miss in his own time, to his discredit). In spite of this, it will be here argued that a momentary glimpse of 'truth' — one pointing to the falsity of our societal values — delivered via abstract creative production can still shine through today, but rarely via artistic production in any traditional sense. Rather, it will be asserted that the interaction of online gaming, the relentless publication of DIY memes, live-streaming and video 'glitches' signal that the game is not yet fully up. Somewhere, or sometimes, the will to create reasserts itself incisively, if only for a short time. In many senses the millennial is the everyman – or 'everywoman' – whose accelerated path to despair positions her to leverage something from within this deeply negative mess we're in. In this singular respect the millennial is Adornian, and *Stranger Things*, made by the millennial generation Duffer Brothers, speaks by analogy of the importance of giving a creative outlet (as with Will Byers' drawings) to even our most irrational seeming visions.

In *Stranger Things Three* the theme of resistance against the shadowy military industrial complex continues as the new 'Starcourt' indoor shopping mall acts as a front for an underground fortress operated by the Soviet military. Beneath the sterile shopping environment of Starcourt the Soviets operate a machine that emits a beam capable of reopening the doorway between the Upside Down and Hawkins, closed in series two.

Meanwhile the mindflayer has possessed a percentage of the population of Hawkins, building a zombie-like army of automatons whose aim is to unify into one huge demogorgon monster, comprised of their flayed innards – united as the rotten parallel to the shallow glitz of the Starcourt Mall, and intent on destroying any last vestige of resistance from Will and his band of perennial saboteurs.

Across town, a 4th July fairground and fireworks display is held by the corrupt neocon Mayor Larry Kline to distract the inhabitants of Hawkins from independent shop closures brought about by the Starmall. Though it cannot stop the mall being torn apart by the twin forces of Russian Sovietism and Capitalism, as they battle Will, Eleven, and company.

Ultimately, it is the creative ingenuity of Will's most hapless friend Dustin, a super-geek who has handcrafted a radio tower, that wins out. As, in the thick of battle with the mindslayer, Dustin sings a rendition of the theme to '80s fantasy movie Never Ending Story to his long distance girlfriend over his makeshift radio tower, we are reminded that for Adorno, as for Marx, the revolution has no end, and only the creatively stubborn will prosper, by sticking together.

What will be ascertained in the following chapter is whether the spiritual-revolutionary paths of the millennial generation's predecessors have been altogether jettisoned, or whether a path to rebellion and self-discovery might exist for the millennial via artistic pursuit. Does the millennial retain something of the doey-eyed or rebellious artist archetype in their genetic makeup? Do we have access into, or better, out of the Upside Down?

Chapter 3

In which we find little hope in the art world

If you want to find out about artists and millennials, and whether any hope exists for either, go to art college. It won't be quite the same as in 1998, or even 1988, when students and professors alike smelt of cigarettes and cheap booze, where every other student appeared to be stoned, and where disdain for authority was the default. But you might still find dreams, and people hatching plots to escape to a better world. Dreams and plots that begin with frantic scribbles and maybe take a more defined form over time. That is, if the student survives the pressure to conform to the contemporary art market.

Most people start out studying an art degree with some idea of why they are doing it, or at the least, with a definition of what art is. This idea may be hard to articulate, not least due to the low self-esteem of the average late teen. It may be expressed more as a feeling, an aspiration, a strong intuition — the kind of things one is encouraged to quickly overcome by the arts education system. By years 2 and 3 of a 3-year bachelor's degree a feeling perhaps best expressed as 'freedom' or 'self-expression' is replaced by a desire to 'interpret the world' to 'entertain' or to expose political injustice.

Smart students by year three will have learned to pander to the exigencies of the market, while those who go on to study a masters and then — with all the luck in the world — sign up to a reputable gallery, will have hardened into agents able to cope with the cynicism of the contemporary art world. Somewhere deep inside of them the sentiment that inspired them to take up art school remains, yet it exists in spite of their arts education, and not because of it. In preparation for a life spent working in the contemporary art world, university turns our notions of what art *is* on their head. This chapter explores the battle between art as a form of self-development and critical inquiry, and art as a mirror of the world that the artist inhabits, complicit with its economic and political forms. Ultimately it asks whether the art world nullifies the creative tendency that might otherwise spur the millennial to challenge the pernicious prevailing political and economic conditions that characterise twenty-first century living.

In some respects the gap between a budding artist's hopes and the realities of the art world is nothing new. Van Gogh's letters contain complaints about the mercantilism of the Paris gallery he had come to work in, while Jean-Michel Basquiat, the famed graffiti artist turned fine art painter, who shot to fame in the '80s complained bitterly of the pressures of art superstardom that eventually led to his death from a heroin overdose, aged 28. Though both of these artists at least went into their careers compelled to follow the spiritual-revolutionary path of the artist. In the twenty-first century it would be very hard to find an emerging artist who still holds the dream in mind. Artistic self-development is the preserve of the Sunday painter, the 'outsider artist' and the mental outpatient, as the market has squeezed out any sense of idealism.

In its time, Basquiat's meteoric rise was the stuff that dreams – whether of the spiritual or material kind – were made of. Born in 1960, as a late Baby Boomer, the artist embodied a vision of authenticity and of striking out at an elitist art world. The son of a middle-class Haitian immigrant father and a mother of Puerto Rican descent, Basquiat grew up in Brooklyn, where he excelled at school and showed promise as an artist from an early age. Aged 16 he began making street art as one-half of graffiti duo 'SAMO' (meaning 'same old shit'), capturing the attention of New Yorkers with scrawled texts that mocked the art scene and mass media of the time: 'SAMO© 4 the SO

CALLED AVANT GARDE; SAMO© AS AN END 2 CONFINING ART TERMS; SAMO© FOR THE SOCIALIZED AVANT GARDE; SAMO© MEDIA MINDWASH, SAMO© AS AN ALTERNATIVE TO PLASTIC FOOD STANDS; MICROWAVE & VIDEO X-SISTANCE- "BIG-MAC" CERTIFICATE FOR XMAS.'

By the age of 20 a mix of cheek, charisma and precocious talent endeared Basquiat to some notable New York personas, not least Andy Warhol, who immediately recognised the younger artist's prodigious skill, and the young Keith Haring, who Basquiat met when he started to hang out at the School of Visual Arts in New York, where Haring was completing a BFA. Basquiat's rise was so fast he had no need to study an art degree, though he did attend the Edward R. Murrow High School, founded upon the pedagogical didactic methods of John Dewey, emphasising interactivity and democracy. Basquiat's formation, however, took place largely in the art world. He was a rare example of an artist that hatched fully formed onto the international art scene.

In 1981 Basquiat earned a stay in residence at the Italian gallerist Emilio Mazzoli's farm, outside Modena, a small city in the region of Reggio-Emilia, after an initial meeting in New York when the merchant was so struck by the young artist that he purchased 20 works for 10,000 dollars and promptly organised Basquiat's visit to the small north Italian city. In Modena, Basquiat would have enjoyed home cooking served at a large table where Mazzoli held court daily in front of an array of A-list Italian artists of the Transavanguardia. For the most part schooled in the Italian academies these artists were more formal than the strange new figure they found in front of them. Mazzoli explains, 'The liberty with which he drew was shocking. Basquiat was rock...loud music, canvas on the floor, spray cans a go-go. A highly instinctive painter.'[12] At times Mazzoli and his wife wondered if Basquiat would deliver, due to his haphazard working schedule. Notwithstanding cultural clashes, at the end of his 2-week residency a show was mounted, albeit to a lukewarm reception. Italy is a bastion of tradition, though beyond that its artists are notoriously 'clicky', sticking to their own friendship groups, which espouse more or less uniform opinions on art, and fighting hard to maintain their positions once they have become established. In spite of this, the show was a sellout, as Mazzoli convinced the local collectors of the value of his protegee. True to the art world, which is populated in part by a close-knit community of investors looking to back the next 'big thing', the impact of those first sales rebounded in New York the following year, when Basquiat sold out his first American solo show at gallery Annina Nosei.

By 1983 he was working in a space that prominent dealer Larry Gagosian set aside below his home in Venice, California and in February 1985 Basquiat featured on the cover of the *New York Times Magazine*. The edition carried an article entitled 'New Art, New Money' in which Cathleen McGuigan discussed the explosion of the art market in the '80s: 'As a result of the current frenzied activity, which produces an unquenchable demand for something new, artists such as Basquiat, Haring or the graffitist Kenny Scharf, once seized upon, become overnight sensations.'[13]

The irony in Basquiat becoming one of New York's hottest commodities in the span of 10 years and after being initially recognised for his anti-corporate anti-art world slogans barely merits pointing out. Though it is worth noting that the highest grossing US box office movie of 1984 was *Beverly Hills Cop*, a film in which off-the-rails and off-duty Detroit police detective Axel Foley (played by Eddie Murphy) exposes corruption at the heart of the Beverly Hills art scene. While managing to make his white colleagues look dumb, the fast-talking African-American Foley exposes gallery owner Victor Maitland's use of art consignments to hide cocaine deliveries (which are in turn disguised as coffee). Avenging the death of his childhood friend in the meantime, Eddie Murphy's portrayal was outstanding in its time (and effectively still is today) for the strength of its black lead character. Though what is often overlooked is the way in which Murphy rights wrongs at the expense of the epitome of white power and corruption: the art world. Unfortunately, however, real life does not echo fiction, at least not in all respects. The art world *is* for sure highly corrupt, though Basquiat — the outsider maverick that promised to unsettle it — ended up being sold out to it. In an essay on Basquiat entitled 'Radiant Child' and appearing in *Artforum* in 1981, Rene Ricard stated, 'To Whites every Black holds a potential knife behind the back, and to every Black the White is concealing a whip. We were born into this dialogue and to deny it is fatuous. Our responsibility is to overcome the sins and fears of our ancestors and drop the whip, drop the knife.' While questioning the sense in asking the 'Black' to drop the knife that was in any case a figment of prejudiced 'White' imagination, one could still ruminate that the proverbial 'whip' has never been dropped.

The signs of burnout from overwork at the hands of his overlords were clear by the mid-'80s, as Basquiat used drugs to deal with the pressures of fame. He suffered paranoia and jealousy — at one point stating that 'It's as if I am just a protégé. As though I wasn't famous before Andy found me' — and was reduced to making samey works to satisfy a hunger for his original vibrant pieces. His eventual overdose in his Manhattan art studio seemed, as so often, like both a suicide and resignation from a position he found untenable: that of superstar artist. With him, the Baby Boomer dream of countering the power base by challenging the symbolic order was dealt a major blow. Thirty years later the art world has not recovered. Rather, Basquiat's treatment appears to have set a perverse standard.

For many people today this is a fact learned at art school, where the heady student expectations of unbound freedom and self-expression — the reason that many went to study art — are met with a crushing reality. Gone are art world high jinks, in favour of 'core professional skills', presentation skills, courses on copyright law, lessons on pricing your artwork and advice on how to ingratiate oneself to the art establishment. This has a further knock-on effect on the art world.

If the battle to assert one's identity against a materialist and bureaucratic art world starts at university, it continues throughout the lives of many artists. While art school smashes the dreams of the budding practitioner, the art world itself is ready to follow up and cash in by processing the most financially promising via a soulless system aimed at minimising artistic risk and maximising profit. If art is about a free play of fantasy, the role of the gallerist is to dash dreams, starting with their own. Indeed, from artists who once entertained notions of free expression to critics who started out wanting to marshal the boundaries of good taste, to gallerists and collectors who formerly held dear to the idea of promoting and buying what they *actually like to look at*, the vast majority of art world players live in a state of abject disappointment. Giving up on your dreams is a prerequisite for success.

Perhaps no one has done more to highlight the ethically dissolute nature of the art world than the late John Berger — critic, novelist and poet — did in *Ways of Seeing*, the book and homonymous BBC TV series of 1972. 'The art of any period tends to serve the ideological interests of the ruling class,' he argued, his eyes penetrating through the TV screen into the homes of an unsuspecting public that was curiously receptive to the news that both high and low culture were a cover for the malintent of the ruling class in Britain. At that point, with the British economy in tatters, the Baby Boomers — the original upstart generation — were beginning to experience a hard landing after the best part of a decade spent high as a kite. Great Britain wasn't San Francisco and free love and hallucinogens were no solution to the problems posed by rising unemployment, a flagging economy and the miners' strikes, which were called one day after the broadcast of the first episode of *Ways of Seeing*, on 12 January.

No longer could one look upon, for example, Gainsborough's portrait of Mr and Mrs Andrews (circa. 1950) as a charming depiction of a couple enjoying rural England: Mr Andrews stood holding his rifle like some kind of public school educated cowboy bearing down on his wife, who is pictured trussed up like a wedding cake. On closer inspection their facial expressions appear sardonic, while their position in relation to the land (*their* land, nonetheless) appears to block the viewer from entry. The painting, which was executed in around 1750, appears as a window onto England's rotten soul. Mr and Mrs Andrews are saying 'keep out!' and the painting they commissioned nearly 40 years before the French Terror is a sign that the ruling elite were not prepared to share their spoils with the masses.

By 9 February 1972 a state of emergency and energy rationing was implemented in the UK due to cold weather conditions and a reduced electric current. Ten days prior to that, the BBC had aired the final episode of *Ways of Seeing*, in which Berger looked at image juxtapositions in magazines in order to throw light on the hypocrisy of the western world, which will happily countenance, for example, an advert for super strength alcohol or bath salts adjacent to images of starving Africans in a glossy magazine spread. Though perhaps more timeless as an image and more universal in its message was the episode's closing sequence, which showed billboard posters urging voters to 'Say Yes to Europe', alongside advertisements for tobacco, Ford cars, tinned fruit, Captain Morgan Rum, Harp lager, the health benefits of cheese, and rail travel. As the sequence cut from billboard to billboard, taking in images of vagrants, passing workers and clothes drying on the balcony of a council house block, Berger's voiceover brought his series to a close with a sense of melancholy befitting the scenery:

'Our cities are papered with pictures of what we might buy, papered with dreams which invite us to enter them, but they exclude us as we now are. Behind the paper are hidden our needs.'[14]

It seems no number of Bacardi beaches can alleviate the gloom of a British city under a slate grey sky, though what stands out about *Ways of Seeing* is the way in which visual culture was implicated as not just an accessory but a principal actor in creating the disappointment, lack and want that characterised British life in the '70s. This is not to say that art is by any means the worst of pursuits and one can think of many more heinous career paths than 'artist': arms trader, people trafficker, politician, to name just three. Though the trouble for art – and by extension visual media in general – is that it enjoys the privilege of being the discipline responsible for expressing dreams. As such, it's going to get hit especially hard when those dreams come crashing down. This is even more the case given art's links to big business, finance and the ruling elite. So long as art maintains a veil of innocence it's going to seem doubly complicit when the veil slips. *Ways of Seeing* was arguably the BBC's most flagrantly leftist moment and certainly remains its most pointed critique of the cultural system in Britain to this day. Since its initial screening and publication as a book it has become a staple of college and university art departments across the world and is regularly referred to by artists as an influence on their work. It remains relevant despite one or two of its televisual sequences appearing embarrassingly dated. When for example, Berger says in episode two of the four-part series (on the 'male gaze') that we might better understand the implications of female nudity in painting by talking to some – (gasp!) – *women*, the sensation is that the viewer at this point is being instructed to recognise Berger's benevolence in so doing. In the ensuing scene a confident cigarette smoking Berger talks to five mostly painfully shy women about female portrayals in art so as to eke out from them a feminist analysis. As cringeful as this scene appears to be, it does take steps towards seeing the exploitation of women in the history of the image as on par with class subjugation: both are undertaken at the behest of powerful men, in conjunction with a compliant or co-opted image maker.

Whatever Berger's failings – and they really belonged to the society he inhabited and found such fault with – his talent for reducing all injustices perpetrated by visual culture to a subjugation of the individual by objective image-making forces (Adorno's 'culture industry' in a nutshell) remains of use when examining contemporary society.

This is crucial as any class, gender or race-based analysis of art risks becoming reduced primarily to a politics of resentment, thereby weakening its critical import. This problem commits the art critic or social theorist to a complicity with injustice of a second order, as her or his critique of the subjugation of people based on their class, gender, ethnicity or sexuality risks appearing as a shrill personal expression of discontent, and as such useless for fostering any collective response to injustice. For this reason, the identification of the impersonal objective forces at play in exploitation are fundamental to a reclaiming of culture, tactically speaking. In so doing we might better understand why we put so much faith in art as a kind of material expression of our inner dreamworld, and how it comes to fail us, generation upon generation.

It would be an understatement to say that finding the right balance between subjective and objective critique is tricky. The issue of how much we credit to the 'I' who looks or acts and how much to the 'she', 'he', or 'it' that is looked at or acted upon is central to cultural, political, humanities and scientific discourse. It is a problem that won't go away precisely because it concerns the conditions that make both human inquiry and interaction possible. Leaving aside the extent to which such a binary mode of reality might be a limitation of human enquiry itself, it is possible to construe the contemporary art world as a field of complex relations between individuals, institutions, art objects and finance mechanisms. At one extreme is the notion of the free individual artist-subject — the path of the spiritual-revolutionary — who creates new realities and is practically untethered by the objective or outer world. At the other extreme reside the materialist-conservative tendencies common to an array of artistic, curatorial and art historical practices, as well as to the activities of financially motivated players. Art, a discipline that arguably has subjective expression as an underlying premise is, one way or the other, remarkably well marshalled, cajoled and subjugated by objective forces that act to keep its message from unbalancing the social status quo. Yet at the same time, some degree of objectivity is required so that artworks can enter into the realm of visibility and exchange rather than existing as esoteric and closed artefacts of self-expression, personal fetish objects, trophies to peculiar personal interests or spiritual whims. Subjectivity and objectivity are, in whatever proportion — to be argued over perennially by philosophers — necessary to one another, in art as in life.

There is a familiar trope in detective films, wherein the killer's lair — often a bedroom — is found filled with objects that pertain to his or her obsession: hair clippings, dolls, shoes, etc. Upon entering, the exclamation, unfailingly voiced by the detective is one of disgust as he or she casts their eyes over a personal display of macabre fetishes. The suspect has kept their 'collection' to themselves, which is in itself arguably a sign of socio-pathological disorder. A body of fetish objects that remains isolated conveys, upon being found, a level of objectivity that is so reductive that it is dangerous to human life. In the movie *Se7en* (1995), the serial killer John Doe (played by Kevin Spacey) shocks Detective David Mills (played by Brad Pitt) as he enters Doe's apartment with Detective Somerset (Morgan Freeman) to find its dimly lit halls playing host to an array of display cases embedded in black, grease covered walls.[15] Objects on display — artfully arranged — include a severed hand from a victim and blood splattered books belonging to another. Se7en was a brutal and cynical film portraying a society with barely any remorse to the individual, yet even within the bleak portrayal of a New York nearly completely lacking in empathy John Doe stands out for the perversity of his materialism. His character is symbolic of the risks inherent in an entirely objective vision of property or people, with complete objectification manifesting in an objectification of people for its own sake (and not for show to others). Yet pure subjectivity would bring about antisocial behaviour of a different order — that of the archetypal 'madman' who, convinced that his or her chosen path is the path for all humanity, proclaims truth in the crowded marketplace. As such, the art world is charged with treading a thin line. The trouble is that the pact that art creates between subjectivity and objectivity is ultimately unconvincing, leading art to embody an antisocial behaviour of a third type — that of the 'con artist'.

The term con artist is applied to people who play tricks on other people's desires, usually as a means of extracting money. While applicable to any field it seems particularly apt to that of politics, where deception appears by now par for the course. This is perhaps because the politician so routinely finds her or himself held to a set of ethical criteria almost impossible to fulfil. In our age of citizen journalism and information leaks, where failures to live up to exacting standards of political life are promptly exposed, the politician is never far from a lie. The same could be said of the arts professional who, in having to convince an audience (or prospective buyer) of the transcendent beauty of an artwork — a beauty that might port us out of the sordid conditions of living — runs up perpetually against the obvious objectivity of the materials they peddle.

It is of course unsurprising that artifice stands at the centre of artistic practice. It is however interesting just how many players are openly and flagrantly involved in maintaining that artifice, and how deeply it extends into professional relations and business dealings that go way beyond the original artifice

committed by the artist's hand. Perhaps principal among these players is the patron or collector, without whom neither the objective material reality or the dreaming capacity of the artist would see the light of day. In Berger's interpretation the art patron occupies both the top of the artworld pyramid and the top of the social pyramid *per se*. As such, via their financial strength they shape art to fit their model of society. What is crucial here is the role of money, which in governing society must also govern art. Accordingly, such art is put to service both in creating and protecting wealth.

Specific activities come to the fore in a given society to the extent to which they are useful in the creation of capital.[16] Consequently, the counter-capitalist tendency in art can only manifest when it is deemed useful to the generation of wealth.

The figure of the collector is fundamental to this course and through a process of commissioning or buying already produced works acts as a guardian of public taste, ensuring that what gets seen will never undermine the profit motive. Now, upon asking a collector how they choose what they buy, one will always be told: 'I buy what I like.' Upon further probing one will find that 'liking' is a gut reaction. A desire to help young or emerging artists will often arise as a further motive for collecting art. However, any time spent with collectors or gallerists reveals that they tend to operate via a kind of spread-betting, whereby they will purchase or promote a number of works from across a range of artists that look set to increase in value in the coming years. What this effectively means is a steady rate of purchases from artists selling in the lower price bracket, who may enter into a higher bracket suddenly and at any given moment. The chance of an artist selling in a low price bracket suddenly achieving a leap in value greatly depreciates with an artist's age. Simply, if an artist hasn't enjoyed commercial success by 50, they are seen as unfit for making sudden profit. Accordingly the exigencies of the market both favour young artists and guarantee that the political content of their work will in no way present a threat to neoliberalism as an economic system. Recognition as an artist is an *a priori* identification of the artist's complicity with capital, and frequently at the expense of more deserving older artists. Though ultimately the co-optation of millennials does not play in their favour as it ties them into a machine in which they are mere minor components, experiencing a life far from that which they dreamed of when they chose to break with more conventional career choices not long before they signed to a gallery and began to sell. Their subjective freedom is put into the service of objectivity, leading to profit for the gallerist and collector, and a continuation of the class conditions of capital.

Italian movie director Paolo Sorrentino's Oscar winning 2014 film *La Grande Bellezza* (The Great Beauty) did much to mock the art world for its exuberance and hypocrisy. A caricature of the decadence of life among the bourgeoise of Italy's capital, the film follows its main character Jeb Gambardella, a one-time successful novelist, as he lives off his fading literary fame going from one seemingly endless salon or terrace party to another. At one point he is invited to a chateau to witness an art performance held in its grounds, involving a child performer who is the daughter of the hosts. An audience comprised of the fallen aristocracy, the *letterati* and contemporary art world aficionados look on as a reluctant girl – no older than 8 years of age – throws and smears paint across a huge canvas. The girl, who nearly refuses outright to engage in the spectacle, looks visibly enraged as onlookers watch approvingly as if witnessing a rare talent. Yet the viewer senses a deception as every semblance of spontaneity appears to have been prefigured. Even the girl's rebellion against her parents has been preordained: in fact, it was the inevitable outcome of the work and the social relations that surround it.

Sorrentino's portrayal is only barely an exaggeration. Stories of artists who are picked up young and subsequently feel pressured by gallerists to perform a role or produce work to order are the norm. The artists themselves are often quite openly derisory about this situation, recounting tales of being asked to 'paint one in the right dimensions to go above a sofa' or 'to produce ten more blue canvases'.

One artist who has enjoyed a meteoric rise while remaining to some extent critical of the system is Colombian born Oscar Murillo, who signed to the highly influential David Zwirner Gallery shortly after finishing his final degree show in 2012 at the Royal College of Art, London, one of the world's most prestigious art colleges. The son of poor immigrants to London, who did not speak English on their arrival, Murillo's works were selling at auction for as much as 401,000 US dollars by 2014 when he was aged just 28. Despite a distinct cooldown in the market for Murillo since then he remains one of the foremost artists to have emerged in the twenty-first century. The works he rose to fame for feature angry scrawled hatchworks of oil paint and oil crayon on canvases that the artist laboured over on the floor of his East London Studio. Made of stitched together canvases and emblazoned with angrily scrawled words such as 'Mango', 'Yoga' and 'Burrito', the works are part action painting and part social critique – bringing to mind an earlier artist of South American descent, Michel Basquiat, mentioned above in Chapter 3. Indeed, Murillo is often compared to his tragic predecessor, a practice that seems both glib and inevitable, with Murillo even having had the same haircut as Basquiat, 'or at the least the movie version,' as Mera Rubell, a collector who is credited along with her husband for discovering Murillo, is quoted as saying.

The Rubells first came across Murillo's work at the Independent art fair in New York in 2012 at the stand of the highly influential London-based gallery Modern Art. Upon seeing that Murillo's works were completely sold out the Rubells contacted gallery owner Stuart Shave who arranged a meeting with Murillo at his studio in Hunter, NY. Following an interview with the Rubells in situ at David Zwirner's gallery, Carl Swanson, journalist and editor-at-large for *NYmag* and *The Vulture* reported in 2014 that:

> Murillo had no work left at his Hunter studio. When Shave told him that the Rubells were visiting, he decided to spend the next two days on a painting bender.
>
> 'We arrive at Hunter at 9 a.m., and he has now painted for 48 straight hours. He hijacked this big space because everyone else had left for Easter holiday,' Mera [Rubells] says.
>
> He looked exhausted after the binge. 'When we met him, we thought he was a homeless person,' says Mera.
>
> 'I immediately held on to my pockets and headed to the door,' says Donald [Rubells].[17]

Aside from portraying the Rubells as aloof from reality, and inappropriate in their attitude towards the artist, this awkward exchange serves to highlight the way in which Murillo has been required to operate as a machine-like component of the art market, much like Basquiat himself. Indeed, it is hard to imagine how troubling the comparisons between Murillo and a man who took his life at least partly because of his inability to process artistic fame must have been for the young artist. But it is also hard to see how Murillo would have achieved his meteoric rise otherwise, not least given the clear fact that he owes so much to Basquiat stylistically.

Notwithstanding his embedeness within the market, Murillo soon began to kick back against a system that sought to categorise him with wit and cynicism. On 14 April, 2014 he opened his first solo show in New York at David Zwirner's gallery, shunning the paintings he had become famous for, in favour of a performative installation comprising a factory line and 13 Colombian workers, who produced chocolate candies throughout the show's 7-week run. The collaboration with Colombian Chocolate manufacturer Colombina references Murillo's family history. Prior to their emigration to London, his mother worked in a candy factory and his father in a sugar processing plant, while several family members still work directly for the 'Colombina' plant.[18] The exhibition, entitled *The Mercantile Novel*, aimed to bring an awareness of the conditions of non-first world factory workers, while at the same time objectifying the privileged art viewing public. While the workers were confined to their working roles, kept away from viewers, who watched their activity on a remote screen, the public were forbidden to enter into the factory area, save for the privileged few. They were, however, able to enjoy wrapped chocolates, emblazoned with a yellow smiley face, evocative of a 'smiley' emoticon. The glibness of the statement was perfectly calculated to critique the shallowness of the art world, though something about it rang hollow for many people. Murillo couldn't hide the fact that he was a vital part in the operation he set out to critique. Of course, one could argue that he deftly ported a class critique into the bourgeois art world. As always, however, it would appear to have been neutralised before it even arrived there.

One wonders if Murillo — still perhaps the world's most prominent millennial artist, having been nominated for the prestigious 2019 Turner Prize — might otherwise have sensed the rottenness of the whole enterprise before he got in too deep and remained just enough of an outsider to critique it convincingly. Though even having failed to do so, all is not lost. We do have, of course, the artist's own rags to riches story to hold on to, though that seems more a validation of neoliberal principles of competition — meritocratic or not — than the concrete functioning of leftist values. Suffice to say, little of the free-spirited revolutionary aspect that one can imagine residing deep within Murillo's psyche is able to shine through the thick veil of objective relations that block his potential message. As clear as it is, it is refracted through layers of irony and self-deprecation on the part of the art world as it excuses itself for its complicity with finance and commerce while digging itself in deeper.

Whether Murillo represents incisive political critique, a type of middle-class voyeurism focused on the lives of workers, or a mixture of both, his career indicates the near impossibility of art coming to public attention while retaining a critical distance. It would seem that the objective tendencies of the art world are vital in bringing an artist to prominence, yet they reduce their best efforts at societal critique to apologies for the wealthy, who increasingly use artworks as a means of investment above all else. This is unfortunately the price paid by the young artist, perhaps more now even than in 1988 when Basquiat took his life. Yet conversely, to follow some kind of emancipatory path in the spiritual-revolutionary vein would likely result in obscurity. The mechanisms of art world power, encompassing the collectorate, the gallery system, the biennale, the fair and the art press are essential to visibility-in-the-world. Though it is perhaps because of this that young creative people need to look elsewhere. While it is unlikely that they will find anything approaching the dreams of emancipation they once held dear when they decided to be 'artists', they may find the path less laden with con men intent on exploiting their sincerity for financial gain. Fortunately for millennials and the generation that follows, platforms for creativity abound outside the art world.

Chapter 4

Keeping up with the cat memes

The Royal Academy Summer Exhibition is a quaint and peculiarly English ritual that – like lawn tennis and the monarchy – somehow ambles along despite seeming long destined for extinction. Each year tens of thousands of hopefuls submit photographs of their works for a fee of £25 to the Royal Academy Summer Exhibition in London for evaluation, from which 4000 are selected for a second round of judging. From there numbers are whittled down until a final selection is chosen for display and offered for purchase in the prestigious space from June to August. The exhibition has been held consistently since 1769, uninterrupted even by two world wars. In that time much has changed, though one thing that remains certain is the presence of cat pictures, which are apparently among the most sold images each year (with 30 per cent of takings from all sold works – feline or not – going to the Royal Academy itself).

The saleability of images of cats explains their wide proliferation in an exhibition which is, after all, held mostly as a fundraising exercise. The Royal Academy's mission – to promote the arts in Britain – is supported by ticket sales, tuition fees for its master's course and submissions and sales money from the annual summer show. That show itself, now in its two-hundred-and-fiftieth year, aims to be as inclusive as possible. As the Royal Academy website boasts, the show 'continues in the tradition of showcasing a variety of work in all media, including painting, sculpture, photography, printmaking, architecture and film', though its reputation is of a dowdy distant relation and forebear to much more radical open shows such as the 'Salons des Refusés' of 1863, which has become an icon of the notion of democracy in the arts, the antithesis to ideals of cultural hierarchy and learned 'good taste'.

The Salon des Refusés was a large-scale exhibition held in Paris displaying works by artists who had been refused entry to the 'Paris Salon', an annual exhibition selected by members of the Academy of Fine Art, which was famously out of touch with emerging modernist trends. In 1863, protests reached the French reigning monarch, Napoleon III, after the majority of submissions to the prestigious show were rejected, including the works of a number of artists today considered to be icons in the canon of art history, such as Gustave Courbet, Édouard Manet and Paul Cézanne. Following the Emperor's intervention (due to a wish neither to be unpopular or to appear out of touch) an alternative space was found for the rejected works in the Palace of Industry, creating great interest among the public, who were keen to see the works of these cultural upstarts.

In his novel *The Masterpiece* (*L'œuvre*, 1886), nineteenth century novelist and chronicler of Parisian life Emile Zola described the scenes at the Salon des Refusés:

> ...from amidst the incoherent ensemble, and especially from the landscapes, all of which were painted in a sincere, correct key, and also from the portraits, most of which were very interesting in respect to workmanship, there came a good fresh scent of youth, bravery and passion. If there were fewer bad pictures in the official Salon, the average there was assuredly more commonplace and mediocre. Here one found the smell of battle, of cheerful battle, given jauntily at daybreak, when the bugle sounds, and when one marches to meet the enemy with the certainty of beating him before sunset.[19]

The exhibition – as Zola vividly conveys – represented something much more than a simple challenge to the cultural order as embodied by the Academy with its preference for staid history, genre and academic portrait painting. The 'battle' that

the novelist describes was not fought merely over representation or stylistic preferences – though these factors were instrumental – but was one of social class and power struggles, continuing the perpetual work of social levelling in a land that had little over 70 years prior to the first Salon Des Refusés seen its ruling elite (and a higher number but lesser total proportion of working class 'anti-revolutionaries') butchered during the revolutionary Terror. That historical episode (responsible for the death of between 17,000 and 40,000 people by guillotine, firing squad, drowning or poor prison conditions) took a number of artists, poets and academics from all backgrounds. With this massacre fresh in the minds of the people of Paris it is unsurprising that Zola turned to the language of war to describe the effect of this exhibition of avant garde artworks. These artists would come to be known as the 'Post Impressionists', one of the most influential art movements of all time. 'On or about December 1910 human character changed,' Virginia Woolf wrote – in her 1924 essay, Mr. Bennett and Mrs. Brown – reflecting on the year of the opening of critic and painter Roger Fry's overview of Post Impressionist art *'Manet and the Post Impressionists'* at the Grafton Galleries in London. Such, in part, was the impact of this relatively new continental art form on the British cultural elite. Though perhaps more than battle or cultural revolution the enduring literary reference of the Post Impressionist period is to a great and bellicose laughter, as the public, struggling to come to terms with the new aesthetic that confronted them, were reduced to fits of hysterics.

Zola's *Masterpiece* documents this phenomenon, as the novel's main character Claude Lantier (based on the novelist's lifelong friend and painter Paul Cézanne) draws close to his work on display at the salon, only to discover that it is the source of the laughter he could hear from several rooms away:

No sooner had visitors crossed the threshold than he saw their jaws part, their eyes grow small, their entire faces expand; and he heard the tempestuous puffing of the fat men, the rusty grating jeers of the lean ones, amidst all the shrill, flute-like laughter of the women. Opposite him, against the hand-rails, some young fellows went into contortions, as if somebody had been tickling them. One lady had flung herself on a seat, stifling and trying to regain breath with her handkerchief over her mouth. Rumours of this picture, which was so very, very funny, must have been spreading, for there was a rush from the four corners of the Salon, bands of people arrived, jostling each other, and all eagerness to share the fun. 'Where is it?' 'Over there.' 'Oh, what a joke!'[20]

Seemingly modelled on the actual public reaction to Manet's *Le déjeuner sur l'herbe* (Lunch on the Grass) featuring two reclining clothed men, a reclining nude woman and a bathing semi-nude woman, Zola's account points to the real and lasting achievement of Post-Impressionist art, with its focus on forms, colours and everyday people. Perhaps there is something extraordinary in Manet's *Le déjeuner sur l'herbe*, which bears some resemblance to the contemporary niche pornographic market 'CMNF' (clothed male, nude female). Though aside from its display of flagrant nudity for its own sake, the real innovation lay in the fact the nude female could have been *anyone* (as opposed to being a figure from Greek myth, for example) — as could the clothed male.

Returning to Woolf's assertion that a change in human character coincided with the opening of Manet and the Post Impressionists it could be asserted that the bright colours, expansive strokes, rhythmic lines and everyday scenes associated with the Post-Impressionist style heralded a kind of democratisation of the arts. In the quasi-folk musicality of the works of the Post Impressionists people began to recognise themselves, thereby bringing about extremes of emotion and above all laughter, an expression often associated with a kind of truce or a relaxing of one's guard in the face of a person or object. The public's laughter in the face of Post Impressionism was one step in a long process that has opened up art to ever wider audiences by releasing the grip of socially exclusive academic conventions on art and its appreciation. Whatever people thought of the 1863 Paris Salon, they didn't need an education in Classics or Theology to understand what they were looking at. They didn't need particularly to understand it at all.

Post Impressionism marked one large step in a process of opening the public to an unadulterated relationship with the artwork, to an immediacy of experience that challenged a prior bourgeois preoccupation with rules and conventions. That process continued with the advent of conceptualism and the notion that *anything* could be art, which is generally traced back to 1914 when Marcel Duchamp declared an upturned bottle rack to be an artwork, and can later be seen in Andy Warhol's presentation of Campbell's Soup tins and Brillo Pad boxes as worthy objects of cultural appreciation. It's a process that has many different strands and histories that won't be analysed in depth here except to say that it's one that was sped up and amplified to a massive (so big as to be unquantifiable) degree with the advent of the internet, which has become a global salon providing the freedom of creative expression and reception that we have idealistically longed for since at least early modernism.

While there are plentiful examples of internet censorship and while surveillance is rife, it remains that more images (including texts) and sounds are being made and consumed (often for free aside from the cost of an internet connection) than ever before. This is as close as we've ever been to the cultural democracy that is often seen to be a pillar of democracy as such, and it is one that on first appearances turns Adorno's analysis of the culture industry on its head, as the public is not only seeing exactly what it wants to see, it is often producing the content. Indeed, Adorno's complaint that an ostensibly democratic system uses mass-produced cultural products to numb the minds of an unsuspecting public loses traction given the vast range of choice and interactivity offered by the internet. At the same time Adorno's hope that art (as in high art, the domain of the middle to upper classes) could expose the societal fallacies conveyed by culture industry products has also become redundant: one effect of *democratisation*'s tendency to reduce art to the status of any other object has been the commodification of art beyond any resistance. Or put otherwise, Adorno's worst fears regarding the homogenising effects of the culture industry have been realised, yet at the expense of the autonomy of high art, which has contradictorily migrated to mass culture in the form of internet memes.

We are not empty vessels buying into a culture industry that has us held captive by the cinema screen or to our TV sets. The internet has undeniably freed us to some greater or lesser extent, making available a vast array of cultural experiences ranging from mainstream to underground to X-rated, to outright criminal. Take for example this random selection of genres on offer from the TV streaming service Netflix: Asian Action Movies; Adult Animation; Brazilian Dramas; Classic Fight-the-System Dramas; Classic Suspenseful Space-Travel TV Shows; Classic War Movies; Slapstick Comedies; Sports Documentaries; Foreign Dramas; Faith and Spirituality Movies; Belgian Movies; Foreign Gay and Lesbian Movies; Romantic Independent Movies; Rock and Pop Concerts; Alien Sci-Fi; Soccer Movies; Political Thrillers; Cerebral French Language Movies from the 1950s; Creature Features from the 1970s; Critically-acclaimed African-American Movies; Mind-bending Japanese Crime Movies; Rockumentaries; and Understated Twentieth Century Period Pieces Based on Books. Yet aside from all this — which in any case presents only a tiny fraction of what is available on one streaming service — there are myriad educational resources, social media applications, music and video streaming sites, finance resources, online games, live streams, message boards, dating sites, and pornography sites available at a click. One could effectively look at all of the aforementioned in a day. One could even (half) read a pdf download of Adorno's *Dialectic of Enlightenment* while doing so.

The notion — ubiquitous in communications studies — of being spoon fed samey productions does not entirely hold up. The majority of leftist academic literature on the media preaches that we don't choose, we only think we do, a point that has lost its meaning and relevance to younger generations. It has begun to sound less like a concern for audience liberty and more like both a moral and aesthetic judgement on the kinds of things people choose for entertainment today. The thing that is perhaps hard for cultural critics to accept is that the proliferation of uncritical, jokey and blasè content on the internet is a direct result of it being the most interactive and democratic media to date. We do choose (so far as choice is at all possible), just not the things that leftist academia has historically expected people to choose when given an immense freedom of choice.[21] Though perhaps the real issue here is the inability of the left to see both the bad and the good in the development of internet media and the particular culture of image production and reception that accompanies it. That is, one can despise the Kardashian-Jenners wholeheartedly but at the same time see the potential in the system that gave them immense cultural power, and which will give power to many other people, and may even eventually break the system of the cultural elite. This is in any case a reality we need to work with.

Fredric Jameson summed up the vast gap between reality and what leftist theorists strive for in *Late Marxism (1991)*: 'The question of poetry after Auschwitz has been replaced with that of whether you could bear to read Adorno and Horkheimer next to the pool.'[22]

Capitalism has so far corrupted society as to make a mockery of leftist theory, so the question is no longer one of whether we have the tools to critique the worst excesses of capital (here 'Auschwitz'), it's one of whether we even care. Today one might ask if it's possible to read Adorno without stopping periodically to look at cat memes.

There are people who really like this predicament and people who hate it, but whether the state of today's visual culture makes you want to laugh or cry it is quite clear that the internet has usurped the art world as a space for free expression and experimentation. It is a giant Salon des Refusés, a more genuinely open Royal Academy Summer Show, featuring both cats and nudity in abundance. Though an unprecedented level of freedom regarding the production and reception of the image may not be a defence in itself of the content being shared. In fact, Adorno had something rather disparaging to say about jokey images displayed in popular media formats that may be of relevance today. Writing in *Minima Moralia* — a book of aphorisms 'on damaged life' — he argues that:

> The pictorial jokes which fill the magazines, are for the most part pointless, empty of meaning. They consist of nothing other than a challenge to the eye of a competition with the situation. Schooled by innumerable prior cases, one is supposed to see 'what's happening' faster than the significant moments of the situation are developing. What such pictures act out, in anticipation of their completion by the well-versed observer, is the throwing of all meaning overboard like ballast in the snapshot of the situation, in the unresisting subjugation to the empty hegemony of things. The state-of-the-art joke is the suicide of intention… Just as the sober-minded gaze, which meets the billboard smile of a toothpaste beauty, perceives the misery of torture in her manufactured grin, so too does

> the death-sentence of the subject, implicit in the universal victory of subjective reason, bristle from every joke and truly every visual representation.[23]

In one paragraph Adorno unwittingly damns a large part of the viral internet, exposing jokey memes and 'toothpaste beauties' as an expression of our hopelessness. The effortlessness of laughter and smiling barely conceals a desperation. It is as if the smile barely conceals a grimace aimed precisely at the indignity of having to always bear that self-same grin.

While of course Adorno could not know just how much watching, for example, *Keeping up With the Kardashians* feels like being hit repeatedly in the face both for its speed and its banality, his sentiment expresses the extent to which the Kardashians are victims as much as perpetrators of the media assault they partake in. It is quite clear that Kim Kardashian West, together with her half-sisters — Kylie and Kendall Jenner — work very hard to achieve the look associated with an effortless life of leisure. Though on the flipside, to pity them would be to lose sight of how much power they wield. It is arguable that the effect of their reality TV show, together with their monetisation of everyday life — as they commodify every aspect of their waking days, snapping it on social media and tagging brands with whom they have sponsorship deals — in some way paved the way for Trump to become President, even in spite of the fact Kim endorsed Hillary Clinton. Indeed, their normalisation of a new level of militant shallowness in the pursuit of profit — recall, for example, that it was Kim Kardashian's manager-mum (the self-styled 'momager') that convinced her to pose for a *Playboy* spread in 2007 — may someday even pave the way for a Kardashian or Jenner presidential campaign (or indeed, a Kanye West campaign). Though even more than this, what Adorno cannot have foreseen is that absolutely nobody is tricked by the Kardashians-Jenners' routine, especially not themselves.

We all know that glib internet memes of cats, comic memes and Instagram models have trapped us in a shallow process of image sharing, reproduction, modification and hollow laughter. And yet, somewhere in all this there is a level of choice and a level of freedom of expression that just doesn't merit being ignored or belittled, and especially not by po-faced philosophers with the social media following of a D-list star at best.

It is worth, for example, bearing in mind that the Kardashian-Jenners' use of social media as a tool for obtaining people's attention has inspired a generation of young women to gain fame and/or notoriety where it wouldn't have otherwise been possible. One such figure is Danielle Bregoli, who shot to fame after appearing on TV psychologist Dr Phill's talk show in September 2016. Invited on the programme with her mother to discuss her bad behaviour (which included routinely hitting her mother and stealing cars), the 14-year-old distinguished herself by picking a fight with the audience with the now immortal line: 'Cash me ousside, how 'bout dat?' The phrase (in plainer English, 'catch me outside, how about that?') became a viral image meme, written above and below the face of Bregoli in the by now familiar meme font. Bregoli has gone on to become an Instagram sensation with 16.5 million followers at the time of writing, under the name Bhad Bhabie, which is also her performance name as she embarks on her career as a rap artist.

Of course this could all seem like a strong indication that society has lost its way, and in many senses it has. People are becoming famous for possessing only trivial skill, or even no skill. In the case of the *Cash me Ousside* meme, the protagonist rose to fame by demonstrating practically the opposite of skill in any formal sense. In fact she became famous for being violent and speaking poorly. However, she represents our desire that anyone can be recognised for their achievements, *or even lack of them.* Bregoli's media savvy turned her from a typically misbehaving teenager to a star in just 11 months (her first single,

These Heaux, was released in August 2017). Though the fact that a poor and rude young woman is getting more attention than, for example, the average academic or artist should not arguably be seen as a disaster. Given the unlikeliness of the situation the same process may well create further ruptures in the cultural status quo, and this can be no bad thing.

It is surely with this spirit of disruption in mind that the hip-hop duo Run the Jewels offered a number of pre-order options for their album *Run the Jewels 2* ahead of its release in 2014. Styled on the extras that a project backer can pay for when funding an initiative on the crowdfunding platform Kickstarter they included, aside from the more conventional offerings of CD, vinyl and t-shirts, the option to pay 100,000 US dollars to have the band avenge a chosen nemesis and 10,000,000 US dollars for the band to retire from music. But it was perhaps the most ridiculous of the extras options that caught the fans' imagination: the band would remix the entire *Run the Jewels Album 2* using cat sounds if the public raised $40,000. Music blogger and call centre employee Sly Jones responded by setting up an actual Kickstarter to collectively raise the money to pay for the musical venture. Shortly after giving his support on twitter, El-P tweeted, 'slowly dawning on me that i might have to make and (sic) album from cat noises'.

As El-P later explained in *Entertainment Weekly*, 'We decided that if there was a way that we could get money to charity, specifically victims of police brutality in America, that it was worthwhile. We figured, hey, f–k it, let's fight injustice with pure, annoying stupidity.'

Meow the Jewels was fully funded before the release of *Run the Jewels 2* with El-P dedicating it on twitter to Michael Brown and Eric Garner, who were, respectively, strangled and shot by police in New York City and Ferguson in 2014. Released in 2015 and featuring a number of guest producers, including Portishead's Geoff Barrow and singer Zola Jesus, the album is somewhat more playful than *Run the Jewels 2*, yet still features a good deal of snarling and clawing at the establishment.

Part joke with deadly serious undertones, El-P told online music magazine *Deadspin,* upon being asked about the album's merits, 'I would never even insult the world by saying "good," but it's certainly the high-water mark for cat-sound records, I think.' Run the Jewels fell prey to two things, the out and out popularity of cat memes and the way in which a daft idea can spiral out of control on the internet.

If the internet has become a Salon Des Refusés, a great exhibition hall for anyone and everyone, what can there be to reject, aside from flagrantly unethical activity? Accept it all – cat memes and 'duckface' selfies included – and something may shine through the fissures in a broken system. 'We know the system is broken but we'll keep on trying anyhow,' has become the oddly Adornian sounding refrain of the millennial. Indeed, Adorno fully perceived the way in which our lack of freedom revolves around the sliver of freedom that we somehow grasp onto (or vice versa). What he arguably didn't grasp is the extent to which freedom and unfreedom could be proportionately amplified and still exist in a relationship with one another.

Chapter 5

In which we find some solace in *Mad Men*

In season 8, episode 1 of *Mad Men* – AMC's phenomenally popular series on advertising executives – Don Draper, the psychopathic ad-man and lead role, finds himself defending the advertising industry to Ron, the male friend (and as it later turns out, lover) of his regular mistress, Midge Daniels. The exchange takes place in a bar bustling with lifestyle beatniks during a poetry recital:

Roy: So what do you do, Don?
Don: I blow up bridges.
Midge: Don's in advertising.
Roy: No way. Madison Avenue? What a gas.
Midge: We all have to serve somebody.
Roy: Perpetuating the lie. How do you sleep at night?
Don: On a bed made of money.
Midge: (wryly) Isn't this an education?
Roy: You hucksters in your tower created the religion of mass consumption.
Don: People want to be told what to do so badly that they'll listen to anyone.
Roy: When you say people, I have a feeling you're talking about thou.
Don: And I have a feeling that you spent more time on your hair this morning than she did. (Gesturing to Midge).
Midge: You two want to head to the urinals and poke it out?
Don: So, Roy, if you had a job what would you do?
Roy: I'm starting a theater, right here in the Village. It's a cooperative.
Midge is going to get in there, paint some flats.

Midge: I said I'd think about it.
Poet girl (sat atop of an upright piano): Last night I dreamed of making love to Fidel Castro in a king-size bed at the Waldorf-Astoria. 'Viva la revolución' he roared, vanquishing my dress.
Outside the window Nikita Khruschev watched us, plucking a chicken.

To a smattering of applause as the collection basket comes around Don says, dryly: 'I should go now. Too much art for me.'[24]

What stands out about this exchange is the extent to which it forms a bond with the viewer, who despite feeling sympathies for Roy – who still harbours some hope for notions of justice, authenticity and truth – ultimately empathises with Don's cynicism. Indeed, *Mad Men*'s phenomenal success is surely in part due to its cold realism, which now strikes a chord with a generation of Netflix viewers too young to have seen its first episodes screened on AMC in June 2007. The role of the media is, after all, to convince the masses to choose against their best intentions, and even against their interests. *Mad Men* performs a kind of immanent critique of the media, demonstrating how unscrupulous the ad-men of the '60s were, both privately and at work, while still managing to get the viewer on board with the culture industry project: to entertain while subjugating. A task made easier given that the alternative – embodied in Roy – is some kind of shrill caricature of resistance, the archetypal freeloader who shuns work and pulls his philosophy from fortune cookies. In reality, Adorno, as critical as he was of the culture industry, would have in many ways been closer to the decadence of Don Draper – without hope – than that of Roy – without a clue. For Adorno, and his brand of negative reasoning (or 'negative dialectics'), an awareness of the near impossibility of surpassing the conditions of domination that have prevailed throughout history was central. The premature circumvention of the conditions of our collective bondage all too easily results in catastrophe as revolution gives way to further subjugation, often accentuated, a point Adorno understood too well as a German Jew exiled from his homeland during Nazi rule. Rather than perpetuate domination, Adorno argued for aesthetic reflection upon novel abstract artworks that, through their estrangement from the world, could open up a glimpse of reality despite the false conditions we exist within, as objects within a rational system of our own making. We created that system to try and temper the force of nature, yet it has come to dominate us as we all fit into the logic of the numerical count. The problem for Adorno was the scarcity of artworks that could withstand and expose the industrial processes that had reduced even humans to numbers. Under the culture industry all becomes akin to advertising. As Adorno and Horkheimer wrote:

> Advertising and the culture industry merge technically as well as economically. In both cases the same thing can be seen in innumerable places, and the mechanical repetition of the same culture product has come to be the same as that of the propaganda slogan. In both cases the insistent demand for effectiveness makes technology into psycho-technology, into a procedure for manipulating men. In both cases the standards are the striking yet familiar, the easy yet catchy, the skillful yet simple; the object is to overpower the customer, who is conceived as absent-minded or resistant.[25]

Though somewhere in the abyss we have become habituated to living within there lays a glimmer of hope even for Adorno. The often quoted line 'It is impossible to write Poetry after Auschwitz,' from Adorno's 1961 essay *On Commitment* is followed later in the same text with the plea that 'literature must resist this verdict, in other words, be such that its mere existence after Auschwitz is not a surrender to cynicism'. Though this may seem both contradictory and somewhat hopeless as a strategy it reveals what Adorno believes art to actually be. For Adorno, art cannot exist after Auschwitz as nothing worthy of being called 'art' can exist in a society that has become so far commodified that even people are treated as objects, systematically worked to death for the war effort, or killed when the cost of feeding them (a paltry amount of food) outweighs the profit their puny bodies can yield. And yet, we must continue to make art anyhow, as via the artwork some glimmer of truth might shine through in our thoroughly controlled and objectified society. Art is something that can shine through irrationally even when the entire weight of rationality (an Enlightenment project gone awry) is assembled against it, yet for the most part what masquerades as art is either a glib pretence aimed at profit, or a shrill opposition to the state of things that serves only to draw attention to them (as with the above-mentioned 'poet girl' from *Mad Men* episode 6 series 1).

Don Draper again seems to be — albeit unwittingly — in parallel with Adorno's thought when, a little after attempting to leave the bar where he is sat with Midge and his love rival, a rendition of *Waters of Babylon* is played by a friend of Midge who she implores Don to stay and listen to. The song, based on *Psalm 137* of the Bible and arranged for music by eighteenth century British composer Philip Hayes was popularised by US pop folk singer Don McLean in 1971 in a rendition not dissimilar to that featured in *Mad Men*. As the song plays we see a close up of an embittered Don Draper cut with images of, respectively, his wife dutifully attending their children and his boss, Roger Sterling, in a hotel with his mistress and secretary. At that moment, Don's face reveals a longing for the stability of a world that will never exist, as the music temporarily cuts through both the drivelling social analysis he has endured from his romantic rival and the facade he is engaged in perpetuating as an ad-man. That Don Draper was so deeply affected by the rendition of *Waters of Babylon* suggests that it was not 'art' that he wished to

get away from in trying to leave the bar. Art, when he actually experienced it, had the opposite effect: it momentarily paralysed him. The problem — and the motive for Adorno's statement on the impossibility of poetry — is that much of what passes for art is unable to momentarily shake the false world view imposed by the auspices of rationality and capital. It is instead a glib substitute that claims to give solace in the face of art's true absence, all the while robbing us blind.

Now, Adorno did not include the *Waters of Babylon* among the artworks (many of them musical) that he considered to be capable of exposing the falsity of societal relations in the mind of the individual subject and it is unlikely that he would have rated it among them. Not least as the text and musical score were written in the service of the Church, which Adorno considered to be in itself a mechanism of domination. Though the scene described illustrates the momentary disruption caused to an established order by the unexpected intrusion into reality of an abstract artistic form (in this case music, the most abstract of the creative disciplines).

For Adorno, it is the modern abstract artwork that momentarily exposes the inherent lie that characterises homogenised and commodified society. As the subject views the modern artwork they may feel 'overwhelmed', thus returning them to a sense of the 'primordial shudder' that the subject felt in the face of unfettered nature before enlightenment forms of domination existed. The modern artwork is capable of producing the effect of that shudder in the subject as a result of its novelty – the bizarre nature of the abstract work is beyond identification by the subject and thereby returns them to a pre-subjective state of being. It is only the novel and unexpected artwork that can produce this result for Adorno, and more particularly the classical works of Arnold Schoenberg (1874-1951) and the writings of Samuel Beckett (1906-1989). As such, any directly or overtly political content is out of the question, as it would revert back into the

negative system of identification. It is, for Adorno, the least political forms of art that have the most political potential.

To add a further contradiction, art's potential in exposing truth via the 'shudder' derives from its being entwined within wider society. The commodification of society frees art from the command of the clergyman, monarch or politician, and this freedom enables art to go one step further in constituting itself as entirely autonomous from society. However, the self -proclamation of art as autonomous from society is ultimately a fallacy, leading Adorno to designate the artwork as a 'fetish'. The 'fetish-character' of the artwork enables it to bring about a criticism of the wider commodification of society whereby everything is defined by its monetary value. Yet it is only ever as a commodity that the artwork finds this at all possible, as it feigns its autonomy from society just as commodities feign a value that goes beyond their form. This has its benefits as it means that the exposure of truth via art is not only possible even within a highly commodified society, it actually needs that commodification to exist in the first place. Adorno's sleight of hand was precisely to embed the conditions of our freedom in those of our bondage.

The question today is whether anything can stand outside the system of exchange long enough to create the kind of momentary shock that jilted Don Draper in the above-mentioned bar scene. For one, if that scene were set in the second decade of the twenty-first century Don's experience would have been interrupted by someone ostentatiously taking a selfie, or by his phone bleeping with incoming messages. Indeed the acts of selfie taking and of messaging — often linked — play into the capitalist machine as our data is mined for sale to companies not unlike the one Draper works for. Adorno would surely argue that platforms such as Facebook are advanced interpretations of the culture industry with their ability to blunt art's capacity far outstripping the movie, radio and print industries of the mid-twentieth century.

At the same time, the relentlessness of digital media culture, along with its attendant hardware (iPhones, iPads, Amazon Fires, Playstation 4, Nintendo Switch, etc) leads the consumer to have to make so many choices that the illusion of freedom becomes constant and unavoidable. Abandoning the paraphernalia that makes such freedom possible, as well as the images and sounds that — in their constancy — act as a mantra of free expression thereby becomes unthinkable. Glimpses of the falsity of such freedom are liable to meet with hostility. Indeed, explaining why a near constant ability to choose what you see and hear from seemingly endless choices, paired with the possibility of free expression in front of an ever-present audience is *not* freedom, is a thankless task. For those who can see through a ruse whereby we have been plugged into a data machine which turns our free time into labour could in any case argue that they are precisely following Adorno's injunction to make 'art' (or receive it) despite the impossibility of so doing, which is in reality what interaction on social media often feels like. Frustratingly, our freedom is by necessity embedded in its opposite.

To be sure, the sense of being absolutely embedded within a system of commodities fronted by a mass media machine is surely as valid now as in Adorno's time (having written and published between the 1940s and 1969 when he died). However, there is undeniably an unprecedented level of interaction within the media with most of what is produced daily being generated by users of media platforms and not their owners. Given this high level of interaction it could be argued that there is an imperative to put out political messages so as to counter the spread of the 'wrong kinds of message' (i.e. racist, sexist, homophobic, anti-muslim and so on). It could also be argued that the mass of constant messages being published across media platforms (both mainstream and new media) leads to a blanket level of abstraction which needs strong and clear figurative and political statements to break through what might otherwise be seen as a stream of sleep, stupidity and nausea inducing gibberish. What new media demands is that we leverage something from within the apparent boundless yet false freedom we occupy, using the available plentiful resources to raise people from the slumber. The jolt or 'shudder' needs to be one that wakes people from a trance induced by the abstraction of life in the digital age, rather than being an abstraction that wakes people from the rigid rationality of the industrial age.

In the twenty-first century, music, memes and game production may help to affect some kind of rupture with the prevailing conditions of capital and the culture industry. Yet if so, it must be a production free from the injunctions to produce *this* or *that* kind of art (figurative or abstract, political or apolitical), rules that seem absurd at a time when creative production is so commonplace, so everyday and integral to self-expression on an ongoing daily basis. To impose rules simply doesn't make sense because the process of identification is practically unavoidable on the one hand, while on the other abstraction has become routine.

Given that all creativity is both controlled and abstracted at source, meaningful or truly 'free' production seems near impossible. It would appear then that the only option we have is to bastardise the mechanisms of capitalist cultural production and reception from within, over and over, knowing always that the machine is too vast, too all-encompassing to overcome entirely. As pieces of that machine, we do have a right to help reconfigure it with shocks and shudders that might reverberate and rejuvenate the audience at least temporarily. That Don Draper moment can still happen, but it may just as easily occur in front of a screen as in a bar and when it does it may be so fleeting as to achieve next to nothing, concretely speaking (and indeed, it was never clear what Adorno's 'shudder' might concretely bring forth anyhow). Might we just have to concede that a balked freedom is a freedom nonetheless and work within the mass of web-based communication that dominates our lives? Whether or not this seems palatable, the world of high art has lost its mantle of progressiveness within visual culture to the YouTube video, the meme, social media and gaming culture. If there is a spiritual-revolutionary path for the millennial perhaps it resides here, in a cynical DIY production of culture that is inextricably tied, via appliances, to the materialist path. Some freedom resides in the myriad choices denied to our forebears.

Chapter 6

The kids are doing it for themselves: but what is 'it'?

Problematically for Adorno's legacy, it is increasingly difficult to conceive of a novel art form capable of creating the illusion of freedom from the capitalist whole. For one, never before seen visual forms (thereby capable of resisting 'identification' and nullification at the hands of rationality) are difficult to come by in an age as image saturated as our own. Though beyond that, images are assimilated within the system of commodities almost as soon as they are produced, either via their marketisation through the art system or, more frequently, via their assimilation into the data and advertising markets of the internet: consequently, an image's first appearance in public generally coincides directly with its commodification. This is barely avoidable with online images, as even a thoroughly novel image finds itself involved in the wider process of monetisation via advertising and data sales due to its being viewed within a browser and often within a social media programme, magazine or news site with featured advertising. In this light even a high degree of abstraction or unintelligibility would be unable to lift an image (either still or in motion) out of the realm of commodification that it practically must inhabit in order to come into being in the world.

Though there are arguably two ways an image can come into being without being immediately co-opted by the capitalist system, both of which intersect in the aesthetic of online memes, DIY videos and creative movements, such as Vaporwave, Seapunk and Witch House.

The first facilitator is technology, either in the form of new hardware, whereby a previously unimagined paradigm for images is created to house the image itself, or in the form of new software technologies, which allow for new forms of image or moving image manipulation. In both cases any accordant novel image is made thanks to the realm of technological development, leading to product design innovation and new hardware and software options being made available for the dissemination of images. The tendency towards the by now ubiquitous 'glitch' aesthetic came about in this way, as increasingly affordable video and photo editing equipment met with increasingly advanced mobile technology, allowing for simple image manipulation apps in which glitch effects — whereby an image appears to be temporarily both 'jammed' and 'blurred' — can be applied to images and video clips. The jilted effect of the glitch, mimicking the failure of '80s analogue technology, for a short time represented a novel language that embodied both nostalgia for a pre-internet age and a sense that the internet — and, by extension, wider society — is 'broken'. The effect is akin to Heidegger's proverbial hammer, that one only becomes aware of when it breaks during use. The manufactured glitch represented a fissure in the internet, with its falsity pointing to the ultimately illusory realm we inhabit. It has now inevitably entered into mainstream advertising as a ubiquitous graphic element.

The second facilitator of an image culture resistant to capital operates by way of an extreme indifference to the societal conditions of commodification. That is to say, within online image culture there is an extreme level of apathy admixed with sarcasm that laughs in the face of the dire social realm we live in, yet equally in the face of any attempt at redemption or transcendence. The production of such image objects suggests that there is a creative element that is still capable of confounding common sense and therefore the process of 'identification', though it doesn't exist in the realm of 'art' as Adorno understood it.

One example of such a creative undertaking is the series of short animations, *Don't Hug Me I'm Scared,* which can be viewed on YouTube. Each of the six episodes (made by artists Becky Sloan and Joseph Pelling between 2011 and 2016 and between 3 and 8 minutes in length) focuses on a theme (including Creativity, Time, Love, Computing, Food and Dreams) approached via three main puppets, which aesthetically resemble *Sesame Street* characters, and a host of others, including inanimate objects that come to life. The series, originally broadcast on the artists' website, has become a cult hit, with the combined programmes amassing several hundred million views. Not much is known about the creators of *Don't Hug Me I'm Scared*, though an interview conducted with the duo along with Baker Terry – who helps out with script writing – in *The Guardian* reveals that the first video was uploaded to YouTube on a whim. Its popularity led Channel 4 to commission a second, while money for four subsequent episodes was found on crowdfunding site Kickstarter.[26]

While precise reasons for the mini-series' popularity are perhaps unclear, it seems its macabre humour, which combines the *Sesame Street* format with scenes of horror and existential crisis, while all the while making self-referential nods to the production process, is key. Four of the episodes begin with the central protagonists – 'Yellow Guy', 'Red Guy' and 'Duck Guy' – sitting together in a typical townhouse setting, and passing the time talking. The world they inhabit is one curiously void of social media, in which time passes slowly, a point sometimes brought to bear by the presence of one or other ticking clock. It is for many older viewers the home of our youth: an '80s Britain prior to widespread internet usage, in which the day was divided between meals and TV. While there is a computer that at points interacts with the trio, both the symbol of the computer and internet are firmly placed within the nexus of existential concerns relevant to the bored and tired human, aware of both their existence and their mortality and confronting them with a warped sense of humour.

In the second episode, a clock situated in the living room

attempts to explain time to Yellow Guy, Red Guy and Duck Guy, taking on a brief and selective journey through the past, before standing on what looks like an oversize film acetate suspended in outer space:

Red Guy: And then what happened after the olden days
Clock: Time went new, got old like history, stuff from the past went into a mystery
Yellow Guy: An old man dies
Clock: But look, a computer, everything's cool...It's a Computer!

From here the show takes a sinister twist, as back in the living room the clock continues, half-singing:

'Look at your hair grow, isn't it strange? How time makes your appearance change...'

This line is accompanied visually with Duck Guy's flesh falling away to the bone as he sits in an armchair, while Yellow Guy, holding a hand mirror, throws his head back screaming and crying (from inside an old style tube TV set in the living room) *'let it stop'*. As the characters return to normal, the clock (now itself inside the TV) declares, 'don't worry, I'm sure you'll be fine, but eventually everyone runs out of time.'

The theme is not dissimilar to those explored by post-war existentialists such as Sartre or Camus. Though what characterises *Don't Hug Me I'm Scared* more than a simple expression of existential doubt is indifference to that doubt. At times funny, at times cruel and often both at once, the perhaps striking feature of the mini-series is that it conveys the extent to which we the viewers have gone beyond even an expression of despair. We are no longer living in the late modern period of dashed utopias and a grievance over their passing, or of the postmodern mourning of the loss of schemas that once made sense. We are not even living in a period of indifference as we await some cataclysmic future event – World War Three or climatic meltdown, even though these things could happen. We are in a period of antipathy towards the political order, but of equal apathy towards any available solution on the left, while the right pushes on with an embrace of the rhetoric of that death cult, 'fascism'.

Under such conditions, individual autonomy (freedom, if one could be so bold) can only be felt via a disdain for the processes of everyday life, yet one that is so monotone and deadpan in its expression as to signal a rebuttal of the historical left – characterised by some kind of yearning for deliverance to paradise – and its creative correlates as much as of the right (even though that is equally disdained).

To explain further, a similarly nihilistic aesthetic can also be seen in Vaporwave music videos. Vaporwave is a DIY music and art movement characterised by a retro aesthetic employing references to popular dance music of the '80s to '00s, consumerism, video gaming and the Windows desktop interface (most often Windows 95, though any retro operating system might suffice). Mixing slowed down beats and samples with pop visuals that sarcastically yet cloyingly reference mass media and consumer culture objects, Vaporwave feels like a movement brought together to plan a party at the end of time. Above all, its kitsch drones have the capacity to frustrate the older listener with their refusal to outright condemn commodification while morosely poking fun at it. As Adam Harper explains in an essay on Vaporwave:

> Wearing manic caffeine grins or concealed enigmatically behind corporate muscle and mirror-shades (or both), musicians such as *Fatima Al Qadiri, James Ferraro, Gatekeeper, INTERNET CLUB, New Dreams Ltd.* and many more are performing the next step in techno-capitalism's disturbing and disturbingly logical sequence. They let flow the music

natics that this category entails.
priation of outsider and counter-hegemonic trends never ending in the contemporary art sphere. In gent Stefan Simchowitz, along with Dublin dealer ; King, sued the young Ghanaian artist (then aged Mahama for breach of contract following a row ks comprised of jute sacks stretched like canvases y the artist. Apparently feeling uneasy at the way pieces — sold in three dimensions 108 by 54 inches, ıes and 72 by 36 inches — would be used to fuel on the artist's work, Mahama withdrew his name ces. After Mahama counter-sued for 'intentional utilation, or other modification of the work,' a settlement was found in 2016 between the parties. en before the original dispute, 27 of the works, vely consisted of sacks mounted on wooden frames, l for an average of $16,700 each.[29]
hese works' values have surely soared. In 2015 the youngest artist on show at the main exhibition enice Biennale, curated by Kenyan Okwui Enwezor, splayed a 3000-metre long pathwork of jute sack *of Bounds* (2015) in one of the show's main exterior s at the prestigious 'Arsenale' site. Mahama's use — which the artist obtains from markets and which y intended for the haulage of cocoa and coal — e complex politics of labour trade in Ghana and er world, yet it became a pawn in a financial game y to the elitism of 'high art'.
ıever know the specifics of the case brought between l Simchowitz and Ellis King, though it signals an ıat has become more brazen than even Basquiat's l have foreseen at the time. It suffices to say that as a growth in websites that rank artists according to value (such as Artrank) or that provide informative

> that lubricates Capital, open the door to a monstrously alienating sublime, twist dystopia into utopia and vice versa, and dare you not to like it.[27]

To take one example, Oneohtrix Point Never's *Nobody Here* (which has 47,524 YouTube hits at the time of writing) features a slowed loop of the line 'there's nobody here', sampled from *Lady in Red* (1986) by Chris de Burgh and played along to the visual accompaniment of a twisting and never ending rainbow road, from the intro to an early '80s laserdisc commercial. *Lady in Red*, which was an ode to the singer's wife, Diane, becomes a hellish metaphor for the world we inhabit. One which promises everything via the image of the rainbow, gives nothing and offers no respite or escape.[28]

Both of these phenomena (*Don't Hug Me I'm Scared* and Vaporwave), while using indifference and sarcasm as a disarming creative tool, are deeply indebted to technology. They are made using readily available editing and mixing software to be used on readily available hardware, at generally affordable prices (not least as the major part of production and editing can now be undertaken on a phone). This in itself shows us that new technology can lead to greater freedom in the dissemination of image and visuals. As Jacques Attali argued in *Noise: The Political Economy of Music* (1977), advances in the production and reception of music (from the court musician, to the concert hall, to the bar room concert or cabaret, to recorded LPs to tapes and then, after the time of Attali's publication, to the mp3, free downloads, YouTube and Spotify) have historically predated and foreseen changes across society. This has been seen recently as mp3 file sharing has led to a revolution in the way we also share video and text. It has led to citizen journalism and to attempted (and sometimes successful) revolutions organised partly over the net. Yet what is so conspicuously absent here is a correlating movement in the 'contemporary arts', in the sense of art made and displayed within the 'art world'.

Indeed, it is remarkable that the entire edifice of the contemporary art world, with its elite procedures, has not come crashing down along with the music and publishing industries. After all, the rhetoric of creative equality comes down from the Salon Refusés, and the European avant garde. Yet, in its social character, art is today perhaps the most archaic meta-genre in existence. Comparatively, and despite their difficulty and inherent elitism, the tools and procedures of music, literature, science, maths, sports, politics, religion have somehow been made more transparent, more readily available to the layman than those that govern art. I do not refer here to the power structure, which is undoubtedly shadowy at best when it comes to the realms of politics and religion, but more to the doorstep, the welcoming point, the entry point of contemporary art which — despite a growth in art making and consumption — remains as barbed and inaccessible as it has ever been. For sure, there are more doors, more museums, more galleries, more biennials and fairs than ever, just as there are more artists and more people in the world. Yet these endless doorways onto art enjoyment and artful employment remain as unwelcoming as ever, as is evidenced in the unfair distribution of art world jobs across the social class spectrum. As a study entitled 'Panic! What Happened to Social Mobility in the Arts?' and carried out in 2015 by Goldsmiths College and the arts organisation 'Create' discovered, 80 per cent of all art world professionals are from middle to higher class backgrounds.

In the face of this we have seen that new tech can innovate in terms of cultural accessibility and it is perhaps this that is needed in order to release us from our deadlock, yet I do not see phenomena such as Vaporwave as leading the way in literally democratising the contemporary art field. Not least as it is not the responsibility of millennial bedroom-as-studio music practitioners to alleviate a centuries old edifice such as the art

world of its decadence. An
have appropriated the aest
softwares used in digital i
Huett with his *Playing Fi*
series *True to Size*, 2016) the
contemporary art so long a
system with its dedication to
bourgeois clique. The forme
YouTube videos made by
men self-consciously pimp
(via bodybuilding). The p
and feminine culture in the
protagonists take two fema
The two passengers watch
series made by a friend of t
between an obsession with r
beauty provide an interest
what is more telling is the c
the protagonists in the vide
they were exhibited within
Geneva, Switzerland). The
which were displayed along
like car parts — to the view
total otherness in respect to
distance between what is de
shown within somehow crea
is ported into a world that i
to the art world. Counterint
cars and cosmetics seems t
in comparison to that of co
emphasis on newness, beau
all, investment. Yet this resp
case earned by porting a no
thus rendering it as 'high ar

based proble
The appr
and causes
2016 the art
Jonathan El
28) Ibrahim
over 294 w
and signed
these simpl
96 by 48 in
speculation
from the p
distortion,
confidentia
However,
which effec
had been s
By now
Mahama w
of the 56th
where he
entitled *O*
thoroughf
of jute sack
are origin
references
with the w
linked clos
One ma
Mahama
art marke
dealers co
we witnes
their mark

> that lubricates Capital, open the door to a monstrously alienating sublime, twist dystopia into utopia and vice versa, and dare you not to like it.[27]

To take one example, Oneohtrix Point Never's *Nobody Here* (which has 47,524 YouTube hits at the time of writing) features a slowed loop of the line 'there's nobody here', sampled from *Lady in Red* (1986) by Chris de Burgh and played along to the visual accompaniment of a twisting and never ending rainbow road, from the intro to an early '80s laserdisc commercial. *Lady in Red*, which was an ode to the singer's wife, Diane, becomes a hellish metaphor for the world we inhabit. One which promises everything via the image of the rainbow, gives nothing and offers no respite or escape.[28]

Both of these phenomena (*Don't Hug Me I'm Scared* and Vaporwave), while using indifference and sarcasm as a disarming creative tool, are deeply indebted to technology. They are made using readily available editing and mixing software to be used on readily available hardware, at generally affordable prices (not least as the major part of production and editing can now be undertaken on a phone). This in itself shows us that new technology can lead to greater freedom in the dissemination of image and visuals. As Jacques Attali argued in *Noise: The Political Economy of Music* (1977), advances in the production and reception of music (from the court musician, to the concert hall, to the bar room concert or cabaret, to recorded LPs to tapes and then, after the time of Attali's publication, to the mp3, free downloads, YouTube and Spotify) have historically predated and foreseen changes across society. This has been seen recently as mp3 file sharing has led to a revolution in the way we also share video and text. It has led to citizen journalism and to attempted (and sometimes successful) revolutions organised partly over the net. Yet what is so conspicuously absent here is a correlating movement in the 'contemporary arts', in the sense of art made and displayed within the 'art world'.

Indeed, it is remarkable that the entire edifice of the contemporary art world, with its elite procedures, has not come crashing down along with the music and publishing industries. After all, the rhetoric of creative equality comes down from the Salon Refusés, and the European avant garde. Yet, in its social character, art is today perhaps the most archaic meta-genre in existence. Comparatively, and despite their difficulty and inherent elitism, the tools and procedures of music, literature, science, maths, sports, politics, religion have somehow been made more transparent, more readily available to the layman than those that govern art. I do not refer here to the power structure, which is undoubtedly shadowy at best when it comes to the realms of politics and religion, but more to the doorstep, the welcoming point, the entry point of contemporary art which – despite a growth in art making and consumption – remains as barbed and inaccessible as it has ever been. For sure, there are more doors, more museums, more galleries, more biennials and fairs than ever, just as there are more artists and more people in the world. Yet these endless doorways onto art enjoyment and artful employment remain as unwelcoming as ever, as is evidenced in the unfair distribution of art world jobs across the social class spectrum. As a study entitled 'Panic! What Happened to Social Mobility in the Arts?' and carried out in 2015 by Goldsmiths College and the arts organisation 'Create' discovered, 80 per cent of all art world professionals are from middle to higher class backgrounds.

In the face of this we have seen that new tech can innovate in terms of cultural accessibility and it is perhaps this that is needed in order to release us from our deadlock, yet I do not see phenomena such as Vaporwave as leading the way in literally democratising the contemporary art field. Not least as it is not the responsibility of millennial bedroom-as-studio music practitioners to alleviate a centuries old edifice such as the art world of its decadence. And while there have been artists that have appropriated the aesthetic of YouTube and of the various softwares used in digital image production (for example Tom Huett with his *Playing Fields, 2014,* or Heather Phillipson's series *True to Size,* 2016) they remain firmly within the realm of contemporary art so long as they inhabit the contemporary art system with its dedication to profit and to serving an international bourgeois clique. The former installation featured edits of staged YouTube videos made by actors posing as young American men self-consciously pimping up their cars and themselves (via bodybuilding). The piece shows extremes of masculine and feminine culture in the US as, at one point, two of the male protagonists take two female passengers for a ride in their car. The two passengers watch and talk about a YouTube makeup series made by a friend of theirs. The contrasts and similarities between an obsession with modding cars and one with hair and beauty provide an interesting object of reflection. However, what is more telling is the contrast between the 'low culture' of the protagonists in the videos and the high culture of the space they were exhibited within (the Center D'art Contemporain in Geneva, Switzerland). The obvious attraction of the videos – which were displayed alongside monochrome panels lacquered like car parts – to the viewer resides in their representation of total otherness in respect to the contemporary art scene. Such distance between what is depicted and the environment that it is shown within somehow creates a momentary relief as the viewer is ported into a world that is somehow innocent in comparison to the art world. Counterintuitively perhaps, the world of show cars and cosmetics seems to be down to earth and forgiving in comparison to that of contemporary art with its impossible emphasis on newness, beauty, class, sophistication and, above all, investment. Yet this respite is only temporary and is in any case earned by porting a non-art environment into an art space thus rendering it as 'high art', with all the economic and class-based problematics that this category entails.

The appropriation of outsider and counter-hegemonic trends and causes is never ending in the contemporary art sphere. In 2016 the art agent Stefan Simchowitz, along with Dublin dealer Jonathan Ellis King, sued the young Ghanaian artist (then aged 28) Ibrahim Mahama for breach of contract following a row over 294 works comprised of jute sacks stretched like canvases and signed by the artist. Apparently feeling uneasy at the way these simple pieces – sold in three dimensions 108 by 54 inches, 96 by 48 inches and 72 by 36 inches – would be used to fuel speculation on the artist's work, Mahama withdrew his name from the pieces. After Mahama counter-sued for 'intentional distortion, mutilation, or other modification of the work,' a confidential settlement was found in 2016 between the parties. However, even before the original dispute, 27 of the works, which effectively consisted of sacks mounted on wooden frames, had been sold for an average of $16,700 each.[29]

By now these works' values have surely soared. In 2015 Mahama was the youngest artist on show at the main exhibition of the 56th Venice Biennale, curated by Kenyan Okwui Enwezor, where he displayed a 3000-metre long pathwork of jute sack entitled *Out of Bounds* (2015) in one of the show's main exterior thoroughfares at the prestigious 'Arsenale' site. Mahama's use of jute sacks – which the artist obtains from markets and which are originally intended for the haulage of cocoa and coal – references the complex politics of labour trade in Ghana and with the wider world, yet it became a pawn in a financial game linked closely to the elitism of 'high art'.

One may never know the specifics of the case brought between Mahama and Simchowitz and Ellis King, though it signals an art market that has become more brazen than even Basquiat's dealers could have foreseen at the time. It suffices to say that as we witness a growth in websites that rank artists according to their market value (such as Artrank) or that provide informative articles next to sales pages (such as Artsy) it ought to come as no surprise that gallerists frequently plan group shows around stock market listings of artists' value, although such a practice rightfully seems repugnant to the average art punter. At a time when *laissez faire* economics have been allowed to infect the art world to such an extent that it has become an apology for neoliberalism, digital media made by kids and young adults with nothing to lose has the edge. Resistance is unwittingly being driven by art world outsiders with computers and a raw urge to explore.

Chapter 7

Lessons from the *League*

There seems to be no end to the daily derision aimed at the millennial generation, particularly for the way they consume media. Glued to their smartphones, PCs and gaming systems, they appear as passive and ethically void entities. At best they are viewed as helplessly beholden to a new virulent strain of media manipulation, at worst they are unwitting acolytes of the new far right. Yet perhaps we are too quick to apply age-old media analyses to phenomena that are wildly removed from the media context they were conceived within. Somewhere in the 'everything's going to hell in a handcart' negativity of the media recipient today there is cause for positivity.

In the twentieth century, interaction with the media amounted to literally talking back at the television. By the second decade of the twenty-first century, talking back at the TV has become making the TV, whether that be via gaming, meme production, the posting of homemade videos or the constant publication of a combination of text, video and still image on social media platforms. Homer Simpson — agitated but essentially apathetic media receptacle — is no longer an accurate model of the media consumer. Instead, Lisa Simpson's saxophone improvisations provide a more fitting account of the new media audience-producer who endures but responds freely to an alienating cultural sphere by producing her own cultural products. This participation can take the form of meme production, gaming, music and video production, video streaming, computer hacking and game design.

Among the forms of internet media most exemplary of the level of free choice we can enjoy today are MOBAs, or Massive Online Battle Arena games, such as *DOTA* (*Defence of the*

Ancients), *DOTA II*, *League of Legends* and *Vainglory*. These free-to-play games (the first two playable on PC or Mac, the latter on mobile devices) feature two teams of five players battling to destroy the opposing team's base, which can be accessed via three principal lanes. Games can be played against computer-controlled enemies ('bots') or real players drawn from across a pool from within your geographical region, while one's own team members will always be drawn from a player pool or be chosen from existing 'friends', giving the games a 'social' aspect. Along the way to the enemy base a succession of towers must be destroyed, while computer-controlled enemy soldiers ('minions') and neutral monsters can be killed for extra gold, which can also be obtained by killing enemy players. That gold can then be spent on weapons, armour, spells and healing potions. The format, which was first seen in a player customised version of *Warcraft III: Reign of Chaos* in 2003, has become hugely popular, with *League of Legends* (released by Riot Games in 2009) boasting over 100 million individual players a month.

Parallel to this, online streaming services such as Twitch and YouTube's dedicated gaming channel attract millions of viewers who watch live streams of individual gamers playing MOBA and other games while commenting in live chat. With a vast network of players interacting globally, the ability to choose from a range of avatars and to strategise gameplay along with fellow gamers from across the continent or world enables a fostering of a form of community, if not the one long envisaged by the political left. Though it must be recalled that, in any case, both Marx and Adorno saw capitalism as potentially providing the impetus and the framework, but not the actual means for emancipation (which would need to arise out of a class consciousness that capital tries to eliminate). Could new media provide a framework for the development of a communal consciousness?

Perhaps the most obvious objection to such a notion is the

issue of bigotry as it relates to gaming and online culture more generally. Studies on the way in which new media reproduces real-world prejudices are commonplace. In 2012, Lisa Nakamura wrote in *Queer female of color: The highest difficulty setting there is? Gaming rhetoric as gender capital* that:

> It is abundantly apparent that the more gaming capital becomes identified with white masculinity, the more bitter the battle over its distribution, possession, and circulation will become. As gaming culture becomes more heavily capitalised both economically and symbolically, it becomes both more important for women to gain positions of power as critics, makers, and players, and more likely that it will be denied.[30]

As much as sexism (for example) is not the literal or sole fault of games or memes, there is a very real sense in which the portrayal of women in gaming reinforces gender stereotypes, with female characters often being clearly sexualised for the pleasure of the male player. Attempts to introduce more varied female roles have been questionable. Blizzard, who developed the first-person team shoot-em-up *Overwatch* (released in 2016) released this statement upon the introduction of the character Zarya — a Siberian weightlifter — to the platform, as a response to fan feedback:

> We've been hearing a lot of discussion among players about the need for diversity in video games. That means a lot of things. They want to see gender diversity, they want to see racial diversity, they want to see diversity along the lines of what country people are from. There is also talk about diversity in different body types in that not everybody wants to have the exact same body type always represented. And we just want you to know that we're listening and we're trying hard and we hope Zarya is a step in the right direction.[31]

While these efforts are laudable, some players in any case have a tendency to sexualise female characters beyond their in-game representation through fan art or 'slash'. *Overwatch* 'slash' – the name given by gaming fans to player created graphics – ranges from crude drawings to more advanced computer-generated graphics and animations, featuring a strong element of pornography centred on the game's female characters. The reddit thread 'Overwatch Porn' showcases a range of gifs, animations, comic strips and still images of female *Overwatch* characters in solo, lesbian and straight sex scenes. So the Chinese climatologist Dr Mei-Ling Zhou, a character who wears glasses and has a generally studious appearance, can be seen spread-legged in a state of partial undress as her thick winter clothes – worn to withstand the cold of her arctic outpost – are cast aside. What this goes to show is that society will port into gaming all manner of bigotry even in spite of developers' and many gamers' wishes to the contrary: Mei-Ling Zhou's hardworking and non-sexualised appearance was taken by a minority of the Overwatch community as an invitation to envisage her as a sexualised object. Troubling as this is, should it overshadow the ability for *Overwatch,* like *League of Legends,* to bring players together from across the world and to allow for unprecedented levels of user choice? After all, these factors may in themselves lead to a development of an altered ethical framework as regards gender and race.

That new media (just as prior mass media) might impose dominant gender values on the masses can come as no surprise. While we must be careful not to disregard such a possibility, we need to hold it in mind jointly with an inquiry into the novel physical relations of power enabled by new media. In so doing we might acknowledge the negative attitudes that shore up class, race and gender divides while recognising the potential for new power relations to emerge. Though is it possible to see new media as both positive and negative simultaneously?

To some extent Adorno and Horkheimer showed us the way here, even though they were decades off interacting with issues of new media, and were too closeted in the realm of white heteronormative academia to address gender, race and sexual orientation themselves.

In the preface to the 1944 edition of the Dialectic of Enlightenment, they state that:

> In the unjust state of society the powerlessness and pliability of the masses increase with the quantity of goods allocated to them. The materially considerable and socially paltry rise in the standard of living of the lower classes is reflected in the hypocritical propagation of intellect. Intellect's true concern is a negation of reification. It must perish when it is solidified into a cultural asset and handed out for consumption purposes. The flood of precise information and brand-new amusements make people smarter and more stupid at once.[32]

Characteristic of Adorno, what is given with one hand is taken away with the other as people's wits are both sharpened and dulled by advanced capitalism. It is worth recalling here that Adorno and Horkheimer, together with the rest of the Frankfurt School, had seen social revolutions and reactions fail epically and disastrously in their own time. It is hardly surprising then that a suspicion of capitalism predominates, leading Adorno's radical negativity to assume the crude binary assessment of the mass media we are familiar with. However, the capacity for the media to make people smarter — albeit with the caveat 'yet stupider' — is hinted at, and here we can sense Adorno's Marxism, as the conditions of global industrialisation, and with it a global right-wing mass media, are seen as providing an infrastructure for the left to hijack. And here Adorno's assertion that 'brand-new amusements make people smarter', along with his admission of 'a paltry rise in the standard of living of the lower classes' should not be overlooked. For it is those improvements that provide the platform for humanitarian gains over time. Hence in the west we enjoy near total literacy and have benefitted from the eradication of a number of fatal childhood diseases, as well as a near 90 per cent use of the internet – giving unprecedented access to information. We might cynically observe that the huge literate population of the west is mere fodder for a right-wing press. That may be the case, but do we then argue that the millions of infants born daily free of the risk of Polio and Smallpox are mere fodder for finance capital? It depends very much on viewpoint and even Adorno wasn't prepared to give up on the possibility of shaping our own perspective to some degree, evidenced by him imploring that we make art even in spite of its impossibility.

The political legacy of the modernist period, which might be best described as a kind of state-capitalist bureaucracy – with its monopoly of force and its massive surveillance capacity – has left us all cynical; reduced by default to an Adornian stance. We see massive social injustice maintained by a cabal. We're aware of the impossibility of toppling the elite, yet we must carry on, so we hope, yet not too much, as hope risks blunting our cynicism, and cynicism helps us feel our edges. Arguably today we are all sympathisers with Adorno, though the younger generations assume this position most naturally, having never had any other kind of revolutionary or transcendental hope to latch on to. Nevertheless, due to advances in technology, the millennial is afforded the possibility of slipping through a wormhole into a shared communal experience whereby a great – infinitesimal – level of choice is given momentarily to them, and on a repeated basis. This is the appeal of meme and gaming culture, which is missed by theorists too eager to use gaming to confirm their critique of social bigotry – a critique that is entirely correct in both its sentiment and targets but does little to help us understand the potential opened up by advances in technology that have made redundant much of the media theory we hold dear.

Indeed, while Adorno's default negativity chimes with today's younger generations, the culture industry model formulated by Adorno and Horkheimer, whereby people are tricked into perceiving that they have a wide choice over the media objects that they purchase or 'enjoy' and which they then passively consume while being brainwashed by the establishment, can no longer be held to be entirely accurate as a description. Perhaps we need to pay heed to the crucial detail in Adorno's critique: media makes people stupid, yes, *yet it makes them smarter too*. What then might be the other inherent contradictions of the media? And particularly new media? Could it make people more isolated, and yet more community based? And should we be ignoring the benefits of smarter, more community-based people, in our negative predilection to see only stupidity and isolation?

The power relations of gaming need to be judged based on what is specific to interactions within gaming, on what it means to exercise choice while being entertained as part of a team as opposed to being passive and often solitary consumers. This, together with the enhanced potential for choice making within new media, should be celebrated and built upon so that the positive aspects of gaming and social media might be deployed as a challenge to negative social phenomena.

Beyond this, it is time to stop berating millennials and their antecedents for failing to take up where we left off: for not solving the problem of bigotry they inherited from us. We should instead see value and take inspiration from their efforts to carve out from within the rotten society they were born into a space for — albeit limited — creative manoeuvre. This is all the more the case given the high stakes behind gaming as an industry with the ability to shape minds. Its potential has not been overlooked by political players of all levels and persuasions aware specifically of how it might sway the attitudes of the millennial generation. The US military, for example, produced their own game series aimed at recruitment of the gaming generation. Entitled *America's Army*, and available for free download on the distribution platform 'Steam', the first-person shooter is heavy on camaraderie, portraying military service as a kind of jaunt undertaken with one's buddies. The franchise, which was first rolled out in 2002 and is currently in its forty-first incarnation as *America's Army: Proving Grounds*, allows potential recruits to explore the realm of battle training alongside other online players. The potential for team play in fostering ideals of community is clearly intentional on the part of the producers, albeit in such a way that might incline the player to take up arms in a literal sense against a future enemy (be they in Afghanistan, Syria, or even Iran).

Such a phenomenon if anything proves the extent to which online gaming is at the forefront of defining community today. It might lead players to come together in a festival of cosplay, whereby they enter into a colourful reenactment of their avatar's exploits. Or it could, conversely, lead players to become soldiers of the world's most belligerent armed force: the US military. Reviews of the game *America's Army* tend to be positive with players noting its completely free system of play, as opposed to many other multiplayer online games, which depend on in-game purchases for revenue: a point which, given the addictive nature of gameplay, with its emphasis on achievements and rewards, could be seen as potentially damaging. Though the omission of any such money trap in *America's Army* comes about as it is backed by the best financed military in the world. There are plenty of indie games with non-aggressive themes available for free or at less than $5 on Steam. And many more that while containing violent motifs do not aim at recruiting players to real-life combat.

Elsewhere the line between gaming interface and real-world play has been effaced entirely, with the US Army recruiting drone operatives from gaming fairs and conventions. The user interface is even reportedly based on games interfaces, with the military taking advice directly from the gaming industry. Though killing human targets situated in Pakistan from the security of a military compound somewhere in Nevada differs greatly from playing war games. Even drone operatives with relatively few direct engagements with the enemy can find their total death tally to be in the hundreds when this information is disclosed upon discharge. In accordance with this burden, incidences of post-traumatic stress disorder among drone operatives are similar to those seen among field combatants.[33]

The role of gaming is not to be taken lightly, and the same of course might be said for meme and selfie production and reception. For this reason, it has itself become something of a battlefield over who we are and who we want to become as a society. One man who saw the potential of online gaming and tried to cash in was Steve Bannon. The former White House Chief Strategist and Executive Chairman of right-wing online newspaper *Breitbart* was for 4 years CEO of Affinity Media (formerly Internet Gaming Entertainment), a company that employed players of games such as *World of Warcraft* to 'farm' in-game treasures and rewards through gameplay, that were then sold to other players. If evidence were needed that gaming tends to take on the character of real-world exploitation, a large number of non-western players were engaged by Bannon to work for low wages playing games so that they could win goodies that were then sold for huge profits to western gamers, with the money going to financial investors.

As a major shareholder in Affinity Media, Bannon had earlier convinced Goldman Sachs (where he formerly worked) to invest $60,000,000 in the company, though its fortunes took a dive amidst a high profile lawsuit taken out by a disgruntled gamer, Antonio Hernandez of Florida, in May of 2007. Hernandez was fed up with the gaming experience being ruined by speculators who diluted the gaming quality by allowing 'noobs' (novice gamers) with money to spoil the gameplay. This added to a drop in revenue as Blizzard, the service that hosted *World of Warcraft*, had since 2006 been clamping down heavily on both the farming and selling of gaming loot, shutting down the accounts of 'gold farmers'.[34] Despite the misadventure, Bannon remained positively moved by his dalliance with massive online games, observing: 'These guys, these rootless white males, had monster power...It was the pre-reddit. It's the same guys on (one of a trio of online message boards owned by IGE) Thottbot who were [later] on reddit.'[35]

What Bannon did not say was that it was similar guys organising via online message boards who had shut down Affinity's mining operations, even if instances of gold farming still persist such as in the sale of *League of Legends* player accounts to save players time in reaching higher levels. In any case Bannon saw a potential army of right-wing acolytes in the millions of disaffected 'white males' who gamed, even if a great many global players were actually non-American, and often non-white!

Becoming Executive Chair of Breitbart News in 2012, Bannon sought to harness the 'monster power' of the 'rootless white male' by appointing one Milo Yiannopoulos, better known simply as 'Milo', as head of the site's Tech Section, which featured a heavy emphasis on gaming and social media. Given the moral conservatism of Milo (a central figure of the alt-right) and his opposition to feminism this appointment helped embroil Breitbart in the series of feuds and harassments that would come to be known as 'gamergate' and which revolved around a disdain for women in the gaming industry. Though it was hardly as if the site needed a rightward push in any case.

It seems clear that Bannon wants to control technologies that might otherwise present hitherto unimagined levels of freedom of expression for the individual, for right-wing ends. In Adornian terms his mistake is to try to identify and control phenomena around him, in keeping with the authoritarian tendency that is inherent in false 'identity thinking'. Who knows what could happen instead if the still gargantuan power of the US recognised in each young citizen a potential indie developer, with the capacity to produce games with greater levels of choice and ever more advanced facilities for fostering community. This can only happen if the wide-open posture of youth and young adulthood is seen as providing opportunity for growth, not exploitation.

For Jordan Peterson, psychologist and ostensibly unwitting new darling of the alt-right, if gaming has any positive potential, it resides in it providing challenges set within rule systems which help to develop skills that are transferable within the wider world.[36] While not untrue, such a careers-adviser mentality misses the potential of free and open play in developing new paths of personal development and social interaction. It also misunderstands the basic rewards of gaming, which do not necessarily come from the fulfilment of tasks and goals inscribed within frameworks of rules that mimic real-world legislation. Yes, games do have rules, though one rarely ever plays them to hone adherence to rule systems. Indeed, that would run entirely against the rationale of 'play', which requires a loss of consciousness of imperatives and restrictions. Arguably absorption in the moment is the real prize of gaming and this could not be more at odds with Peterson's injunctions laid down to the millennial as he implores them to grasp the weight of history and myth. Peterson's mistake here can be most clearly elucidated by looking to his one mention of Adorno in his *12 Rules of Life*, Chapter 7, in which the reader is advised to 'pursue what is meaningful, not what is expedient'. In the chapter Peterson explores the darkness of the human soul arguing that we need to take personal responsibility for our comfort, accepting all that is wrong (or right) in human existence and then going on to create 'meaning' in life one small step at a time, by alleviating small discomforts and unnecessary evils. Such advice for living is of course sound to an extent, even if it differs little with the innumerable self-help books that have for decades jostled with the philosophy sections of our bookstores for shelf space. It is not the practical advice that Peterson gives around the good sense in keeping a daily routine or in 'tidying one's bedroom' that I personally take issue with. That kind of advice has been passed from generation to generation for all of history, only to be largely ignored until experience eventually attests to it being wholly sensible. It is the worldview that underpins Peterson's advice that renders it suspect. To further elaborate, with regard to Adorno, Peterson states, quite incorrectly: '"After Auschwitz," said Theodor Adorno, student of authoritarianism, "there should be no poetry." He was wrong. But the poetry should be about Auschwitz.'[37]

Of course Adorno said no such thing. As already stated, he said that the conditions for making art are impossible in light of what humanity had clearly become on the path to and passage throughout the Second World War and its worst excesses. That descent for humanity accorded for Adorno with the path of rationality being pursued to a perverse degree, such that humans became mere fodder for the capitalist war machine. It is against this that art must be brought forth using all our resources of irrationality, so as to make of it a deception even greater than that played out by capitalism. If the numbers machine that is today's finance banking makes people debt slaves, art is capable of saying 'I see no debt, I see only a human', so long as the art is not itself thoroughly commodified. It is art's job therefore to bring forth chaos (as resistance to a stifling rationale), a point that Peterson fundamentally opposes later in the same chapter when he says: 'Meaning is what is put forth more powerfully than mere words can express by Beethoven's "Ode to Joy", a triumphant bringing forth from the void of pattern after pattern after beautiful pattern, every instrument playing its part, disciplined voices layered on top of that, spanning the entire breadth of human emotion from despair to exhilaration.'[38]

This contrasts with Adorno's own use of Beethoven's *Ode to Joy* in *Aesthetic Theory*, his last unfinished work:

> The experience of art as that of its truth or untruth is more than subjective experience: It is the irruption of objectivity into subjective consciousness. The experience is mediated through subjectivity precisely at the point where the subjective reaction is most intense. [...] It [Beethoven's 9th Symphony] resonates like an overwhelming 'Thus it is'. The Shudder is a response coloured by fear of the overwhelming. By its affirmation the music at the same time speaks its truth about untruth.[39]

For Adorno, Beethoven's music shocks the individual viewer (or subject) into a realisation of its true link to nature as the 'irruption of objectivity into consciousness' or the overcoming of the false boundary between rule-based human culture and the chaotic and deadly auspices of nature. What abstract art does (and music is the most abstract of the arts) is disarm our tools for distancing the threat of nature. We might ask 'why would you do that?' Though for Adorno it is those same tools that humanity has inadvertently turned against itself as a kind of technocratic tyranny. Beethoven's symphony was not an attempt to make everything alright by reinstating the harmony of nature via a group of well-synchronised orchestral players. Its power resides in making everything appear *all wrong*, such that we might realise the fallacy of social conditions in any case.

Peterson argues that meaning is provided by a balance between chaos and order, yet such thinking always comes from the purview of an 'order' which has already deemed itself superior to chaos, otherwise there would be no grounds to ever assume the possibility of a balance in the first place. So his advice that we should do what is meaningful, not what is expedient, assumes that keeping a daily routine that includes tidying your room and doing good deeds for strangers can intervene at a metaphysical level to temper the disorder of existence itself. For Adorno it is precisely such moralising that leads to tyranny for its arrogant assumptions that there is an order that can be instilled upon nature. Rather, that 'order' is a human fallacy that exists alongside myriad other factors within nature.

If this all seems rather far from gaming, it is worth asking what kind of gamer one wants to be? One who rigidly adheres to rules at the expense of gameplay? Or one capable of inventing new games from old ones through a process of creative reinterpretation? And imagine what tools the latter approach would give to our youngest generations. Here it may be worth visiting the millennia old game of chess, which is rigid with rules passed down from generations. It is, without doubt, a great game for honing one's strategy, as Peterson would surely agree. Though it is singularly useless in the teaching of genuine cunning or creativity. Indeed, there are people who will never enjoy chess so long as they don't get to change the rules as they go along. These are the people that introduce *Star Wars* or lego figurines onto the board just as they sense loss, or who at some point send the whole board hurtling through the air, only to rearrange the pieces on the board's blank underside: effectively the 'Upside Down' of *Stranger Things*, referenced back in Chapter 1. And in many ways these people have every reason to behave as they do when faced with a game that is fundamentally untruthful in respect of the conditions of life. Who can deny that there is truth in the underside of the chess board?

I see twenty-first century Aesthetics as occupying that underside and the millennial as the master of its gameplay. It is an abstract realm that Adorno might have approved of, even despite his distance from the pluralist trends of meme making and gaming. Above all, the instrumentalisation of the millennial by Bannon and Peterson can be seen as aligned with a shrill moral panic spread about the times we live in: '*our freedom will derail us!*' Its antidote resides in a refusal to let the right-wing seize the technologies ideal for the free dissemination of ideas and images, and use them for tyranny.

We have no hope. Let's keep hoping.

Endnotes

1 That is to say, that while western foreign policy has arguably always been inherently cynical, today there is not even an attempt to appear to pursue an ethical framework for intervention overseas on the part of western governments. This arguably came about precisely because information is so readily available as to render useless any efforts at feigning a 'just' foreign policy. Following the mainstream media exposure of the bare-faced deception by President George W. Bush and Prime Minister Tony Blair concerning weapons of mass destruction leading to the Iraq War, sites such a Wikileaks have laid bare the profit motive of conflict operations. As argued in Adam Curtis' documentary *Hypernormalisation* (2016), the response of western governments is to promote a base level of confusion such that in Syria, for example, we do not even know who we are fighting with or against. For the Baby Boomer and Generation X-er there was at least a pretence of ethical responsibility to which to hold governments accountable (such as the fight to end the scourge of 'godless communism').

The inexistence of any such ethical radar today puts distance between the millennial and her or his forebears.

2 Theodor Adorno and Max Horkheimer. *Dialectic of Enlightenment* (Verso, 1997), 123.

3 Charles Harrison and Paul Woods. *Art in Theory, An Anthology of Changing Ideas, 1900-2000* (Blackwell Publishing, 2003), 760-764.

4 Ben Cosgrove. "The Invention of Teenagers: LIFE and the Triumph of Youth Culture," Time Magazine, 2013, http://time.com/3639041/the-invention-of-teenagers-life-and-the-triumph-of-youth-culture/.

5 Jon Savage. *Teenage*. DVD. Directed by Matt Wolf. Cinereach:

New York. 2014.

6 There are no fixed generational boundaries just as there are no fixed boundaries to define, for example, social class or gender. The earliest birth year for millennials varies between 1978 and 1982, with the latest varying between 1996 and 2004. William Strauss and Neil Howe give the following dates for post-war generations: Baby Boom Generation (1943–1960); Generation X (1961–1981); Millennial Generation (1982–2004). However, Harvard's Joint Center defines millennials as being born from 1985–2004. With variations occurring widely one can only broadly define a generation, with crossovers inevitable. Ultimately it is the impact of technology and social and political events that define a given generation.

7 . *Generation Zero.* Directed by Steve Bannon. Citizens United: Washington D.C. 2010.

8 Annie Kelly. "Children as young as seven mining cobalt used in smartphones, says Amnesty," The Guardian, 2016. https://www.theguardian.com/global-development/2016/jan/19/children-as-young-as-seven-mining-cobalt-for-use-in-smartphones-says-amnesty

9 Jeremy W. Peters. 'Bannon's Worldview: Dissecting the Message of "The Fourth Turning,"' The New York Times, 2017. https://www.nytimes.com/2017/04/08/us/politics/bannon-fourth-turning.html.

10 Jordan Peterson. *12 Rules for Life: An Antidote to Chaos* (Penguin Random House, 2018), 51.

11 Jordan Peterson. *12 Rules for Life: An Antidote to Chaos* (Penguin Random House, 2018), Kindle edition, 48-50.

12 Anna Ferri. "Anche Basquiat E' Stato Qui", Converso, 2014. http://www.conversomag.com/anche-basquiat-e-stato-qui/.

13 Kathleen McGuigan. "New Art, New Money," New York Times, 1985. https://archive.nytimes.com/www.nytimes.com/books/98/08/09/specials/basquiat-mag.html.

14 *Ways of Seeing*. "Episode Four." Directed by Michael Dibb. Written by John Berger. BBC Two, January 29, 1972.

15 *Se7en*. DVD. Directed by David Fincher. New Line Cinema: New York. 1995.

16 As Marx argues in his Economic and Philosophic Manuscripts of 1844: "The extent to which money, which appears as a means, constitutes true power and the sole end – the extent to which in general the means which turns me into a being, which gives me possession of the alien objective being, is an end in itself...can be clearly seen from the fact that landed property, wherever land is the source of life, and horse and sword, wherever these are the true means of life, are also acknowledged as the true political powers in life."

17 Carl Swanson. "Oscar Murillo Perfectly Encapsulates the Current State of the Contemporary Art World," Vulture, 2014. http://www.vulture.com/2014/06/oscar-murillo-perfectly-represents-contemporary-art-world.html.

18 Karen Wright. "In the studio with Oscar Murillo, artist," The Independent, 2013. https://www.independent.co.uk/arts-entertainment/art/features/in-the-studio-with-oscar-murillo-artist-8803147.html

19 Emile Zola. *The Masterpiece* (Pearl Necklace Books, 2015), Kindle edition, chapter 5.

20 Emile Zola. *The Masterpiece* (Pearl Necklace Books, 2015), Kindle edition, chapter 5.

21 Ultimately the issue of choice is a subject for philosophical study. Though as it is colloquially taken the act of choosing is the act of following through on a preference. If then, it can be stated that there was very little choice open to the media audience in the mid-twentieth century, given both the lack of available options and the homogeneity of the products on offer, it must be conceded that there is relatively *more* choice today, given both the wider choice and greater interactivity on offer.

22 Fredric Jameson. *Late Marxism* (Verso, 1996), 248.
23 Theodor Adorno. *Minima Moralia* (Verso, 2005), 141.
24 *Mad Men*. "The Hobo Code." Series One, Episode Four, Directed by Phil Abraham. Written by Chris Provenzano. AMC, September 6, 2007.
25 Theodor Adorno and Max Horkheimer, *Dialectic of Enlightenment* (Verso, 1997), 163.
26 Will Coldwell. "Don't Hug Me I'm Scared: the puppets who sing, dance and eat raw meat," The Guardian, 2016. https://www.theguardian.com/culture/2016/jan/27/dont-hug-me-im-scared-youtube-viral-puppet-show-interview
27 Adam Harper. "Vaporwave and the pop-art of the virtual plaza," Dummymag, 2012. https://www.dummymag.com/features/adam-harper-vaporwave
28 Adam Harper., "Why Oneohtrix Point Never is our Artist of the Year," Dummymag, 2010. https://www.dummymag.com/Features/2010-why-oneohtrix-point-never-is-our-artist-of-the-year
29 Sarah Douglas and Andrew Russeth., "Jute Sack Artworks Are at the Center of Simchowitz Lawsuit Against Venice Biennale Artist," Artnews, 2015. http://www.artnews.com/2015/08/25/jute-sack-artworks-are-at-the-center-of-simchowitz-lawsuit-against-venice-biennale-artist/30 Lisa Nakamura. "Queer female of color: The highest difficulty setting there is? Gaming rhetoric as gender capital," Journal of Gender, issue no. 1 (2011): 4.
30 Lisa Nakamura. "Queer female of color: The highest difficulty setting there is? Gaming rhetoric as gender capital," Journal of Gender, issue no. 1 (2011): 4.
31 Patricia Hernandez. "New *Overwatch* Character Shows Blizzard Really Is Listening," Kotaku, 2015. https://kotaku.com/new-overwatch-character-shows-blizzard-really-is-listen-1689904549
32 Theodor Adorno and Max Horkheimer. *Dialectic of*

Enlightenment (Stanford, 2002), xxvii.

33 Roy Wenzl. "The kill chain: inside the unit that tracks targets for US drone wars," The Guardian, 2018. https://www.theguardian.com/world/2018/jan/23/the-kill-chain-inside-the-unit-that-tracks-targets-for-us-drone-wars

34 John Dibbell. "The Decline and Fall of an Ultra Rich Online Gaming Empire," The Wire, 2008. https://www.wired.com/2008/11/ff-ige/

35 Mike Snider. "Steve Bannon learned to harness troll army from 'World of Warcraft,'" USA Today, 2017. https://eu.usatoday.com/story/tech/talkingtech/2017/07/18/steve-bannon-learned-harness-troll-army-world-warcraft/489713001/

36 Jordan Peterson. "Are video games like World of Warcraft bad for you?" YouTube video, 08:32. Posted February 2018. https://www.youtube.com/watch?v=kzbGUDKCajk

37 Jordan Peterson. *12 Rules for Life: An Antidote to Chaos* (Penguin Random House, 2018), Kindle edition, 218.

38 Theodor Adorno. *Aesthetic Theory* (Continuum, 1997), 238.

39 Theodor Adorno. *Aesthetic Theory* (Continuum, 1997), 244.

References

Adorno, Theodor and Horkheimer, Max. *Dialectic of Enlightenment*. New York: Verso, 1997.

Adorno, Theodor and Horkheimer, Max. *Dialectic of Enlightenment*. Stanford, California: Stanford University Press, 1997.

Adorno, Theodor. *Minima Moralia*. New York: Verso, 2005.

Adorno, Theodor. *Aesthetic Theory*. London: Continuum, 1997.

Attali, Jacques. *Noise: The political economy of music*. Vol. 16. Manchester University Press, 1985.

Bannon, Steve. *Generation Zero*. Citizens United: Washington DC 2010.

Berger, John. *Ways of Seeing*. "Episode Four." Directed by Michael Dibb. BBC Two, January 29, 1972.

Coldwell, Will. *"Don't Hug Me I'm Scared: the puppets who sing, dance and eat raw meat." The Guardian*, 2016. https:// www.theguardian.com/culture/2016/jan/27/dont-hug-me-im-scared-youtube-viral-puppet-show-interview (accessed November 14, 2017).

Cosgrove, Ben. "The Invention of Teenagers: LIFE and the Triumph of Youth Culture." Time Magazine, 2013. http://time.com/3639041/the-invention-of-teenagers-life-and-the-triumph-of-youth-culture/ (accessed September 9, 2018).

Curtis, Adam. *Hypernormalisation*. Directed by Adam Curtis. BBC iPlayer, October 16, 2016.

Dibbell, John. "The Decline and Fall of an Ultra Rich Online Gaming Empire," The Wire, 2008. https://www.wired.com/2008/11/ff-ige/ (accessed June 12, 2018).

Douglas, Sarah and Russeth, Andrew. "Jute Sack Artworks Are at the Center of Simchowitz Lawsuit Against Venice Biennale Artist." Artnews, 2015. http://www.artnews.com/2015/08/25/jute-sack-artworks-are-at-the-center-of-simchowitz-lawsuit-against-venice-biennale-artist/ (accessed January 10, 2013).

Ferri, Anna. "Anche Basquiat E' Stato Qui." Converso, 2014. http://www.conversomag.com/anche-basquiat-e-stato-qui/ (accessed January 13, 2018).

Fredric, Jameson. *Late Marxism*. New York: Verso, 2007.

Green, Joshua. *Devil's Bargain: Steve Bannon, Donald Trump, and the storming of the presidency*. Penguin, 2017.

Harper, Adam. "Vaporwave and the pop-art of the virtual plaza." Dummymag, 2012. https://www.dummymag.com/features/adam-harper-vaporwave (accessed November 14, 2017).

Haw, Brock. *The Greatest Generation*. Chicago: University of Chicago Press, 2007.

Hernandez, Patricia. "New Overwatch Character Shows Blizzard Really Is Listening." Kotaku, 2015. https://kotaku.com/new-overwatch-character-shows-blizzard-really-is-listen-1689904549 (accessed December 3, 2017).

Kelly, Annie. "Children as young as seven mining cobalt used in smartphones, says Amnesty." The Guardian, 2016. https://www.theguardian.com/global-development/2016/jan/19/children-as-young-as-seven-mining-cobalt-for-use-in-smartphones-says-amnesty (accessed May 30, 2018).

Masnick, George. "Defining the Generations Redux." Joint Center for Housing Studies of Harvard University, 2017. http://www.jchs.harvard.edu/blog/defining-the-generations-redux/ (accessed June 5, 2018).

McGuigan, Kathleen. "New Art, New Money." The New York Times, 1985. https://archive.nytimes.com/www.nytimes.com/books/98/08/09/specials/basquiat-mag.html (accessed December 11, 2018).

Nakamura, Lisa. "Queer female of color: The highest difficulty setting there is? Gaming rhetoric as gender capital." *Ada: A Journal of Gender, New Media, and Technology* 1 (2012). (Accessed online at: http://www.bgsu.edu/content/dam/BGSU/college-of-arts-and-sciences/ics/documents/Nakamura_Final.pdf on November 17, 2017).

Peters, Jeremy. "Bannon's Worldview: Dissecting the Message of 'The Fourth Turning,'" The New York Times, 2017, https://www.nytimes.com/2017/04/08/us/politics/bannon-fourth-turning.html (accessed June 15, 2018).

Peterson, Jordan. "Are video games like World of Warcraft bad for you?" YouTube video, 08:32. Posted February 2018. https://www.youtube.com/watch?v=kzbGUDKCajk

Peterson, Jordan. *12 Rules for Life: An Antidote to Chaos*. Penguin Random House, Kindle edition, 2018.

Provenanzo, Chris. *Mad Men*. "The Hobo Code." Series One, Episode Four, Directed by Phil Abraham. AMC, September 6, 2007.

Snider, Mike. "Steve Bannon learned to harness troll army from 'World of Warcraft," USA Today, 2017. https://eu.usatoday.com/story/tech/talkingtech/2017/07/18/steve-bannon-learned-harness-troll-army-world-warcraft/489713001/ (accessed July 20, 2018).

Strauss, William, and Howe, Neil. *The fourth turning: What the cycles of history tell us about America's next rendezvous with destiny*. New York: Three Rivers Press, 2009.

Swanson, Carl. "Oscar Murillo Perfectly Encapsulates the Current State of the Contemporary Art World" Vulture, 2014. http://www.vulture.com/2014/06/oscar-murillo-perfectly-represents-contemporary-art-world.html (accessed January 13, 2018).

Wenzl, Roy. "The kill chain: inside the unit that tracks targets for US drone wars," The Guardian, 2018. https://www.theguardian.com/world/2018/jan/23/the-kill-chain-inside-the-unit-that-tracks-targets-for-us-drone-wars (accessed June 10, 2018).

Wolff, Michael. *Fire and Fury: Inside the Trump Whitehouse*. New York: Henry Holt, 2018.

Wright, Karen. "In the studio with Oscar Murillo, artist." The Independent, 2013. https://www.independent.co.uk/arts-entertainment/art/features/in-the-studio-with-oscar-murillo-artist-8803147.html (accessed January 16, 2018).

Zola, Emile. *His Masterpiece*. Pearl Necklace Books. Kindle edition. 2015.

CULTURE, SOCIETY & POLITICS

Contemporary culture has eliminated the concept and public figure of the intellectual. A cretinous anti-intellectualism presides, cheer-led by hacks in the pay of multinational corporations who reassure their bored readers that there is no need to rouse themselves from their stupor. Zer0 Books knows that another kind of discourse – intellectual without being academic, popular without being populist – is not only possible: it is already flourishing. Zer0 is convinced that in the unthinking, blandly consensual culture in which we live, critical and engaged theoretical reflection is more important than ever before.

If you have enjoyed this book, why not tell other readers by posting a review on your preferred book site.

Recent bestsellers from Zero Books are:

In the Dust of This Planet
Horror of Philosophy vol. 1
Eugene Thacker
In the first of a series of three books on the Horror of Philosophy, *In the Dust of This Planet* offers the genre of horror as a way of thinking about the unthinkable.
Paperback: 978-1-84694-676-9 ebook: 978-1-78099-010-1

Capitalist Realism
Is there no alternative?
Mark Fisher
An analysis of the ways in which capitalism has presented itself as the only realistic political-economic system.
Paperback: 978-1-84694-317-1 ebook: 978-1-78099-734-6

Rebel Rebel
Chris O'Leary
David Bowie: every single song. Everything you want to know, everything you didn't know.
Paperback: 978-1-78099-244-0 ebook: 978-1-78099-713-1

Cartographies of the Absolute
Alberto Toscano, Jeff Kinkle
An aesthetics of the economy for the twenty-first century.
Paperback: 978-1-78099-275-4 ebook: 978-1-78279-973-3

Malign Velocities

Accelerationism and Capitalism

Benjamin Noys

Long listed for the Bread and Roses Prize 2015, *Malign Velocities* argues against the need for speed, tracking acceleration as the symptom of the ongoing crises of capitalism.

Paperback: 978-1-78279-300-7 ebook: 978-1-78279-299-4

Meat Market

Female Flesh under Capitalism

Laurie Penny

A feminist dissection of women's bodies as the fleshy fulcrum of capitalist cannibalism, whereby women are both consumers and consumed.

Paperback: 978-1-84694-521-2 ebook: 978-1-84694-782-7

Poor but Sexy

Culture Clashes in Europe East and West

Agata Pyzik

How the East stayed East and the West stayed West.

Paperback: 978-1-78099-394-2 ebook: 978-1-78099-395-9

Romeo and Juliet in Palestine

Teaching Under Occupation

Tom Sperlinger

Life in the West Bank, the nature of pedagogy and the role of a university under occupation.

Paperback: 978-1-78279-637-4 ebook: 978-1-78279-636-7

Sweetening the Pill

or How We Got Hooked on Hormonal Birth Control

Holly Grigg-Spall

Has contraception liberated or oppressed women? *Sweetening the Pill* breaks the silence on the dark side of hormonal contraception.

Paperback: 978-1-78099-607-3 ebook: 978-1-78099-608-0

Why Are We The Good Guys?

Reclaiming your Mind from the Delusions of Propaganda

David Cromwell

A provocative challenge to the standard ideology that Western power is a benevolent force in the world.

Paperback: 978-1-78099-365-2 ebook: 978-1-78099-366-9